Table of Contents

jQuery Mobile: Up and Running

Maximiliano Firtman

O'REILLY®

Beijing · Cambridge · Farnham · Köln · Sebastopol · Tokyo

jQuery Mobile: Up and Running

by Maximiliano Firtman

Published by O'Reilly Media, Inc., 1005 Gravenstein Highway North, Sebastopol, CA 95472.

O'Reilly books may be purchased for educational, business, or sales promotional use. Online editions are also available for most titles (*http://my.safaribooksonline.com*). For more information, contact our corporate/institutional sales department: (800) 998-9938 or *corporate@oreilly.com*.

Editor: Simon St. Laurent
Production Editors: Jasmine Perez and Teresa Elsey
Copyeditor: Linley Dolby
Proofreader: Stacie Arellano

Indexer: Lucie Haskins
Cover Designer: Karen Montgomery
Interior Designer: David Futato
Illustrator: Robert Romano

February 2012:   First Edition.

Revision History for the First Edition:
2012-02-07   First release
See *http://oreilly.com/catalog/errata.csp?isbn=9781449397654* for release details.

ISBN: 978-1-449-39765-4

[LSI]

1328541205

Preface

This book is the ideal companion for web designers and developers wanting to create mobile experiences using jQuery Mobile.

jQuery Mobile has appeared in the market to solve one problem: dozens of mobile platforms and browsers and the need to create compatible interfaces for all of them.

This book requires just basic knowledge of HTML (any version), and basic JavaScript is helpful for the last chapters. The reader doesn't need to understand HTML5, JavaScript, or jQuery to use most of the jQuery Mobile framework and the contents of this book.

Conventions Used in This Book

The following typographical conventions are used in this book:

Italic
> Indicates new terms, URLs, email addresses, filenames, and file extensions.

`Constant width`
> Used for program listings, as well as within paragraphs to refer to program elements such as variable or function names, databases, data types, environment variables, statements, and keywords.

`Constant width bold`
> Shows commands or other text that should be typed literally by the user.

`Constant width italic`
> Shows text that should be replaced with user-supplied values or by values determined by context.

 This icon signifies a tip, suggestion, or general note.

This icon indicates a warning or caution.

Using Code Examples

This book is here to help you get your job done. In general, you may use the code in this book in your programs and documentation. You do not need to contact us for permission unless you're reproducing a significant portion of the code. For example, writing a program that uses several chunks of code from this book does not require permission. Selling or distributing a CD-ROM of examples from O'Reilly books does require permission. Answering a question by citing this book and quoting example code does not require permission. Incorporating a significant amount of example code from this book into your product's documentation does require permission.

We appreciate, but do not require, attribution. An attribution usually includes the title, author, publisher, and ISBN. For example: *"jQuery Mobile: Up and Running* by Maximiliano Firtman (O'Reilly). Copyright 2012 Maximiliano Firtman, 978-1-449-39765-4."

If you feel your use of code examples falls outside fair use or the permission given above, feel free to contact us at *permissions@oreilly.com*.

Safari® Books Online

Safari Books Online is an on-demand digital library that lets you easily search over 7,500 technology and creative reference books and videos to find the answers you need quickly.

With a subscription, you can read any page and watch any video from our library online. Read books on your cell phone and mobile devices. Access new titles before they are available for print, and get exclusive access to manuscripts in development and post feedback for the authors. Copy and paste code samples, organize your favorites, download chapters, bookmark key sections, create notes, print out pages, and benefit from tons of other time-saving features.

O'Reilly Media has uploaded this book to the Safari Books Online service. To have full digital access to this book and others on similar topics from O'Reilly and other publishers, sign up for free at *http://my.safaribooksonline.com*.

How to Contact Us

Please address comments and questions concerning this book to the publisher:

O'Reilly Media, Inc.
1005 Gravenstein Highway North
Sebastopol, CA 95472
800-998-9938 (in the United States or Canada)
707-829-0515 (international or local)
707-829-0104 (fax)

We have a web page for this book, where we list errata, examples, and any additional information. You can access this page at:

http://shop.oreilly.com/product/0636920014607.do

To comment or ask technical questions about this book, send email to:

bookquestions@oreilly.com

For more information about our books, courses, conferences, and news, see our website at *http://www.oreilly.com*.

Find us on Facebook: *http://facebook.com/oreilly*

Follow us on Twitter: *http://twitter.com/oreillymedia*

Watch us on YouTube: *http://www.youtube.com/oreillymedia*

## CHAPTER 1

The Mobile Platform

If you are reading this book, you are probably a web designer or a web developer, maybe a jQuery fan or a webapp developer. Before coding, we need to address the mobile ecosystem and where jQuery Mobile fits into it. Let's do it.

Why Do We Need jQuery Mobile?

The first question that you should be asking yourself is *why does jQuery Mobile exist?* Why do we need something special for mobile devices if there are plenty of mobile browsers rendering standard desktop websites?

To answer these questions, let me copy and paste some extracts from my other book *Programming the Mobile Web* (O'Reilly). By the way, I asked for permission from myself for doing that.

Myths of the Mobile Web

As the Web has moved onto mobile devices, developers have told themselves a lot of stories about what this means for their work. While some of those stories are true, others are misleading, confusing, or even dangerous.

It's not the mobile web; it's just the Web!

I've heard this many times in the last few years, and it's true. It's really the same Web. Think about your life. You don't have another email account just for your mobile. (Okay, I know some guys who do, but I don't believe that's typical.)

You read about the latest NBA game on your favorite site, perhaps ESPN; you don't have a desktop news source and a different mobile news source. You really don't want another social network for your mobile; you want to use the same Facebook or Twitter account as the one you used on your desktop. It was painful enough creating your friends list on your desktop, you've already ignored many people...you don't want to have to do all that work again on your mobile.

So, yes...it's the same Web. However, when developing for the mobile web we are targeting very, very different devices. The most obvious difference is the screen size, and yes, that will be our first problem. But there are many other not-so-obvious differences. One issue is that the contexts in which we use our mobile devices are often extremely different from where and how we use our comfortable desktops or even our laptops and netbooks.

Don't get me wrong—this doesn't mean that, as developers, we need to create two, three, or dozens of versions duplicating our work. This is where jQuery Mobile comes to the rescue.

You don't need to do anything special when designing for the mobile web

Almost every smartphone on the market today—for example, the iPhone and Android-based devices—can read and display full desktop websites. Yes, this is true. Users want the same experience on the mobile web as they have on their desktops. Yes, this is also true. Some statistics even indicate that users tend to choose web versions over mobile versions when using a smartphone. However, is this because we really love zooming in and out, scrolling and crawling around for the information we want, or is it because the mobile versions are really awful and don't offer the right user experience? I've seen a lot of mobile sites consisting of nothing but a logo and a couple of text links. My smartphone wants more!

One website should work for all devices (desktop, mobile, TV, etc.)

As we will see, there are techniques that allow us to create only one file but still provide different experiences on a variety of devices, including desktop, mobile, TV, and game consoles. This vision is called "One Web." Today, there are a lot of mobile devices with very low connection speeds and limited resources—non-smartphones—that, in theory, can read and parse any file, but will not provide the best user experience and will have compatibility and performance problems if we deliver the same document we would for the desktop. Therefore, One Web remains a goal for the future. A little additional work is still required to provide the right user experience for each mobile device, but there are techniques that can be applied to reduce the work required and avoid code and data duplication.

Just create an HTML file with a width of 240 pixels, and you have a mobile website

This is the other fast-food way to think about the mobile web. Today, there are more than 3,000 mobile devices on the market, with almost 50 different browsers (actually, more than 500 different browsers if we separate them by version number). Creating one HTML file as your mobile website will be a very unsuccessful project. In addition, doing so contributes to the belief that the mobile web is not useful.

Mobile Webapps

I'm not going to enter the discussion about mobile web development versus native development. In fact, I believe that the discussion is mostly wrong. Often the discussion is about native code versus JavaScript code or browser apps versus installed apps. However, what these discussions fail to mention is that multiplatform development is quite a challenge in the native development environment because each platform requires a different SDK. Therefore, because the real concerns are ease of development and deployment to multiple mobile devices, mobile web development is a perfect solution for most situations. The term *webapp* has plenty of synonymous or similar concepts, such as mobile webapps, widgets, hybrids, HTML5 apps, and more.

In particular, a mobile webapp differs from typical mobile websites in its purpose. A webapp typically has a more transactional way of thinking in the user interface, emulating native mobile applications. It is still created using web technologies (HTML, CSS, JavaScript, AJAX) but offers an application-similar experience to the user.

Frequently mobile webapps also make use of HTML5 features, such as offline or geolocation access, to provide a better experience. Geolocation is not an official part of the HTML5 specification, but a W3C API of its own; however, it is often mentioned under the HTML5 umbrella.

A webapp can be implemented in many ways (as shown in Figure 1-1) including:

- Accessed from the browser
- Installed as a full-screen webapp
- As an installed webapp via a package officially implemented by vendors (sometimes called widgets)
- As an installed webapp embedded in a native application, commonly known as hybrid

We will cover how to create these webapps in the rest of the book. For more in-depth information, just cross the street to my other book: *Programming the Mobile Web* (O'Reilly).

A webapp typically generates new challenges for web designers and developers, such as loading views instead of pages, maintaining a two-way navigation between views, and creating rich controls specifically for touch devices.

So, Again...Why Do We Need jQuery Mobile?

If you read the last few pages (and I'm pretty confident you did), you are aware that mobile web design and development presents new challenges for us. We need to create webapps that are more than simple websites; there are too many devices out there with different browser compatibilities; and there are also too many libraries trying to solve the same problem with mixed community and device support.

Figure 1-1. A webapp delivered as (from left to right) a browser-based experience, a full-screen installed application, and an embedded webapp inside a native app (hybrid)

That is why jQuery Mobile was created: to help designers and developers create mobile web experiences easily, and for those experiences to be multiplatform, customizable, and with unobtrusive code.

The extensive worldwide jQuery community also provides a great opportunity for the framework's future.

The framework has received official sponsorship and support from many of the biggest companies in this area, including the following:

- Adobe
- Mozilla Corporation
- HP Palm
- BlackBerry/RIM
- Nokia
- DeviceAtlas and dotMobi

What Is jQuery Mobile?

According to an official note at *http://www.jquerymobile.com*:

> jQuery Mobile is a unified user interface system across all popular mobile device platforms, built on the rock-solid jQuery and jQuery UI foundation. Its lightweight code is built with progressive enhancement, and has a flexible, easily themeable design.

What jQuery Mobile Is Not

To understand jQuery Mobile, it is very important to know what it is not.

jQuery Mobile is not a jQuery alternative for mobile browsers.
> To use jQuery Mobile, you need to include the typical jQuery framework. It is not a replacement; it is a UI layer on top of jQuery.

jQuery Mobile is not a webapp SDK.
> You can create the whole mobile experience with jQuery Mobile but you will need some additional work to compile it as native apps. We will see how, why, and when to do this in the next chapters.

jQuery Mobile is not a framework for JavaScript lovers.
> Except in the case of certain advanced topics, you won't need any JavaScript code for jQuery Mobile to work. That is great if you are a web designer who hates all of those braces and semicolons.

jQuery Mobile is not the solution for all mobile applications, websites, or games.
> However, it covers solutions for most of them. For the others, well...I have to convince you to read my other book somehow.

The Framework

If you don't know what jQuery is, you may be a time traveler from 10 years in the past. If you are Marty McFly, point your browser to *http://jquery.com* and read about this incredibly useful JavaScript framework, the most used one on the Web since 2007.

jQuery Mobile is a framework that delivers webapp experiences to mobile and tablet devices, mainly with touch interfaces, effortlessly, across multiple platforms, and using only HTML5 standard code. A jQuery Mobile app looks like Figure 1-2.

The platform uses the jQuery "core" framework, a JavaScript library, a CSS 3 stylesheet, and some resource images.

jQuery Mobile is comparable to jQuery UI on the desktop side: it's just a UI framework. The name (without any UI inside) leaves you to wonder whether it's a core framework; but I believe the decision was made to take advantage of the power of the jQuery trademark inside the designer and developer world.

 The framework was created by the same team as the main jQuery framework, whose leader is John Resig, JavaScript Tool developer for the Mozilla Corporation (@jeresig on Twitter).

This new platform, like jQuery and jQuery UI, was released as an open source project under a dual license MIT or GPL version 2.

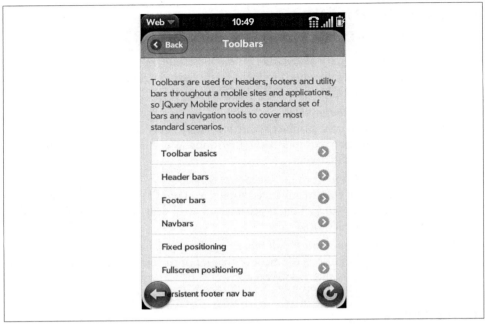

Figure 1-2. A typical jQuery Mobile webapp with standard theming in smartphones, a webOS device in this case

 If you want to participate in the development, you can provide patches, fix bugs, participate in the discussion, and work over the active live code on *http://jquerymobile.com/contribute*.

The Mobile and Tablet World

People do not browse the Web only from their desktop. Now we have very different devices with different screen sizes, input mechanisms, and even new features from old friends such as HTML, JavaScript, and CSS.

Mobile devices are here. There is no doubt—there are more than five billion devices worldwide and counting. Tablets are also coming in a big way, with millions in the market.

Device Categories

Right now, we can divide mobile devices into the following categories:

- Mobile phones
- Low-end mobile devices

- Mid- and high-end mobile devices, also known as social devices
- Smartphones
- Tablets

Mobile phones

Okay, we still have mobile phones in some markets. These are phones with call and SMS support. They don't have web browsers or connectivity, and they don't have any installation possibilities. These phones don't really interest us; we can't do anything for them right now.

In a couple of years, because of device recycling and evolving services provided by carriers and manufactures, such phones will probably not be on the market anymore.

Low-end mobile devices

Low-end mobile devices have a great advantage: they have web support. They typically have a very basic browser, but this is the gross market. Perhaps they aren't the most heavy Internet users today, but this may change quickly with the advent of social networks and Web 2.0 services. If your friends can post pictures from their mobile devices, you'll probably want to do the same, so you may upgrade your phone whenever you can.

Nokia, Motorola, Kyocera, LG, Samsung, and Sony Ericsson have devices for this market. They typically do not have touch support, have limited memory, and include only a very basic camera and a basic music player.

Mid-end/high-end mobile devices

This is the mass-market option for a decent mobile web experience. Mid-end devices maintain the balance between a good user experience and moderate cost. In recent years, this category was also known as social devices, meaning that the users access social sites, such as Facebook or Twitter via the mobile web.

In this category, devices typically offer a medium-sized screen, basic HTML-browser support, sometimes 3G, a decent camera, a music player, games, sometimes touch, and application support. The big difference between these and smartphones is that high-end devices generally are not sold with flat Internet rates. The user can get a flat-rate plan, but he'll have to go out and find it himself. Starting in 2011, many of these devices include WLAN (WiFi), as we can see in Figure 1-3.

Smartphones

There are dozens of smartphone devices on the market, including iPhone, Android-based devices, webOS, Symbian, BlackBerry, and Windows Phone (Figure 1-4). This is the most difficult category to define. Why aren't some mid-end and high-end devices

Figure 1-3. The Nokia X3-02 Touch and Type: a mid-end touch device, with numeric keypad and WiFi

considered "smart" enough to be in this category? The definition of *smart* evolves every year. Even the simplest mobile device on the market today would have been considered very smart 10 years ago.

Typically when you buy a smartphone, you sign up for a one- or two-year contract with a flat-rate data plan. A smartphone, as defined today, has a multitasking identifiable operating system, a modern HTML5 browser, wireless LAN (WLAN, also known as WiFi) and 3G connections, a music player, and several of the following features:

- GPS (Global Positioning System) or A-GPS (Assisted Global Positioning System)
- Digital compass
- Video-capable camera
- TV out
- Bluetooth
- Touch support
- 3D video acceleration
- Accelerometer

Figure 1-4. A sampling of smartphone devices

 Some multimedia devices qualify as smartphones for us web creators, but they don't have a phone feature. On this list are the Apple iPod Touch and the Sony PlayStation Portable (PSP). The only difference from tablets is their screen size, less than three inches.

Tablets

A tablet is a device with a large screen (between 6 and 11 inches), a full HTML5 browser, WLAN connection (WiFi), sometimes 3G, touch support, and all the other features that we can find on a smartphone.

In this category, we can find many devices, including the following:

- Apple iPad
- Samsung Galaxy Tab
- BlackBerry PlayBook
- Barnes and Noble Nook Color
- Motorola Xoom
- LG Optimus Pad
- Amazon Fire
- Sony S1 and S2

Operating Systems and Browsers

This book is not intended to delve deeply into the mobile ecosystem. There is a detailed list of operating systems, platforms, and browsers in *Programming the Mobile Web*

(O'Reilly). However, if we are going to create mobile web experiences, we need to at least know what we are talking about.

In the mobile world, we can divide the operating systems in two main groups: identifiable operating systems and proprietary ones. In the latter group, we will find mainly phones, low- and mid-end devices.

With the identifiable operating systems, we will be more interested in which OS a device has than its brand and model. I mean, we are not going to develop a webapp for the Samsung Galaxy; we are going to develop a webapp for Android devices. The iPhone may be an exception to this rule, because it is a platform of its own, having as of this writing only one device: the iPhone. (Different versions of the device are just that; for web developers there are no huge differences between an iPhone 4 and an iPhone 3GS.)

Table 1-1 lists the operating systems we can find on today's market in smartphones and tablets.

Table 1-1. Operating systems and browsers available in smartphones, social devices, and tablets

Operating system	Creator	Browser included	Other browsers
iOS	Apple	Safari	Opera Mini and pseudo-browsers
Android	Google	Android Browser	Firefox, Opera Mini, Amazon Silk, Opera Mobile
Symbian	Nokia	Symbian Browser	Opera Mini, Opera Mobile
webOS / Open webOS	HP (formerly Palm)	webOS Browser	
Windows Phone	Microsoft	Internet Explorer	
Windows Mobile	Microsoft	Internet Explorer	Opera Mobile
MeeGo	Nokia	Micro Browser/Nokia Browser	Firefox
BlackBerry OS	RIM	BlackBerry Browser	Opera Mini
Tablet OS	RIM	Tablet OS Browser	
S40	Nokia	Nokia Browser	
Bada	Samsung	Samsung Browser	

Every operating system has different versions, and some allow the user to update to a newer one. Every OS comes with an installed browser, but the user can install and use an alternative browser. Sometimes the manufacturer or the operator from whom the user bought the device installs or replaces the default browser with an alternative, such as Opera Mobile.

If we expand our browser research to low- and mid-end devices, we will find more than 20 other new browsers, including Ovi Browser, NetFront Browser, and Phantom Browser from LG. But that is not the target of jQuery Mobile right now.

What Is a Pseudo-Browser?

A pseudo-browser is a native application that users can install on their devices. They use the same engine as the default browser, but offer extra features over it. There are plenty of examples for iOS, such as SkyFire or Perfect Browser. They all use Safari as the final rendering engine; therefore, for jQuery Mobile, they are not separate browsers.

In *Programming the Mobile Web*, you will find 20 pages with detailed information about browser types and features of each one.

jQuery Mobile Compatibility

jQuery Mobile is a framework intended for touch devices, including smartphones, tablets, and multimedia devices. The compatible list will change with time and as the framework continues to evolve, so it is difficult to publish a complete list here.

The jQuery Mobile 1.0 version is compatible with the following by-default browsers:

iOS
> Safari for iPhone, iPod Touch, and iPad from iOS 3.2

Android OS
> Android Browser phones and tablets

BlackBerry OS
> BlackBerry Browser for smartphones from 5.0 and for tablets

Symbian
> Nokia Browser for touch devices

webOS
> webOS Browser from webOS 1.4

Bada
> Bada Browser

MeeGo
> Micro Browser and Nokia Browser (included in Nokia N9)

Windows Phone
> Internet Explorer from Windows Phone/Mobile 6.5 and Windows Phone 7.0

Kindle
> Browser from Kindle 3

jQuery Mobile is also compatible with the following third-party browsers:

- Opera Mini, fully supported from 5.0 on most devices
- Opera Mobile, fully supported from 10.0 on most devices
- Firefox Mobile

This compatibility list just gives you some information to start with. The compatibility is far more complex than this list because we can cross multiple operating system versions with multiple browser versions with different results. Even newer devices not listed here will be compatible with the library if they support the minimum features that the framework needs.

To simplify: jQuery Mobile will work on every browser with the capabilities to offer the experience that the framework provides. Any modern browser should be included in this list.

 Many modern mobile browsers use a WebKit-based engine, like Safari or Chrome for desktop. Any modern WebKit-based mobile browser should be fully compatible with jQuery Mobile. Also Chrome, Firefox, Safari, Opera, and Internet Explorer for desktop are compatible with jQuery Mobile.

Mobile graded browser support

jQuery Mobile uses a table chart to define the compatibility of every device with this library (Figure 1-5). I would not try to enter in this categorization war if I were you. But you can check it if you want more information at *http://jquerymobile.com/gbs/*.

 Many modern desktop browsers, such as Firefox, Google Chrome, Safari, or Internet Explorer, are compatible with jQuery Mobile too. Even if it is not intended for desktop applications, this ability will be useful for testing purposes. However, we will see later that installing an emulation environment will be useful.

I believe the compatibility is far more complex than this table, and for a typical web designer and developer it should be absolutely hidden. There are better ways to know if a feature is available in a mobile browser than trying to categorize each one of them. One solution is right in your hands: *use jQuery Mobile*.

GBS (Graded Browser Support) divides mobile browsers into three categories: A-grade, B-grade, and C-grade. In the jQuery Mobile world, here's what these grades mean:

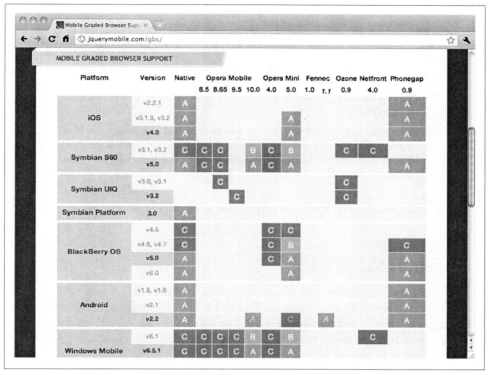

Figure 1-5. jQuery Mobile maintains a list of browser compatibility on its website

A-grade

A browser with CSS3 media queries capability. These browsers will be fully tested by the jQuery team. However, some features will be automatically disabled if the device does not support them. The framework provides a full experience with AJAX-based animations.

B-grade

Browser has an enhanced experience but without AJAX navigation features.

C-grade

A browser incompatible with jQuery Mobile. This browser will not receive any CSS or JavaScript code from the framework, so the user will see a plain HTML file with the content. We will see later in this book how to handle this situation.

PhoneGap and native development

If you look into the Mobile Graded Browser Support Table of jQuery Mobile, you will find PhoneGap as a browser. PhoneGap is not a browser; it's a framework with which to create hybrids. That is: native applications with a webapp inside. PhoneGap is officially supported by jQuery in many platforms, such as iOS, Symbian, BlackBerry, Android, and webOS.

The great news is that you can use whatever hybrid framework you like; jQuery Mobile will work if it works for PhoneGap. That is because PhoneGap is not a browser by itself; it is just a framework using the native browser engine.

To make it simple: *jQuery Mobile is compatible with the creation of native apps with HTML.*

HTML5 and CSS3

I know most web designers and developers panic about HTML5 and CSS3. Before saying anything about it: don't worry, jQuery Mobile will make everything for you. Therefore, you don't need to know HTML5 or CSS3 to work with this framework. I encourage you to learn them regardless. You will be able to accomplish much more knowing these new standards, but that is for a later discussion.

This book is not intended to teach you HTML5 or CSS3, but it is important to understand some things about them. Many mobile browsers, mainly inside smartphones and tablets, support HTML5, CSS3, and other APIs.

I can talk for hours about HTML5, including its history and what it has to offer to the mobile space.

HTML5 in hard terms is an evolving standard that includes changes to the HTML markup and lot of new APIs in JavaScript (yes, HTML5 is a lot about JavaScript APIs). HTML5 in a more casual term is an umbrella for many modern features inside browsers, including the W3C's formal HTML5 standard, other W3C APIs, CSS3, and nonstandard extensions. You can check *http://mobilehtml5.org* for compatibility information for HTML5 in mobile browsers.

jQuery Mobile uses many of HTML5 features to provide a great and fast experience on mobile browsers. That does not mean that the browser needs to support HTML5 as a whole. In fact, many old browsers still support some HTML5 markup even without knowing its existence. jQuery Mobile uses CSS3 a lot, when possible, for animations, gradients, effects, and UI rendering.

To further arouse your curiosity, with HTML5, CSS3, and other modern techniques, you can provide, with or without a jQuery Mobile experience, the following features:

- Offline access
- Offline storage
- Web sockets
- Geolocation access
- Accelerometer and gyroscope support
- Animations
- 2D and 3D transformations
- Gradients and visual effects
- Viewport management (for zooming support inside the browser)
- Webapp installation metadata
- Integration with native applications
- Multimedia support
- Graphic drawing (vector and bitmap)
- Custom font support

There are several samples and links regarding these features on my blog, *http://www.mobilexweb.com/*.

Main Features

jQuery Mobile started in August 2010 as a modern framework, including many patterns and best practices for multiplatform development. The main features of the framework are:

- Cross platform, cross device, and cross browser
- UI optimized for touch devices
- Themeable and customizable design
- Usage of nonintrusive semantic HTML5 code only, without the need of any Java-Script, CSS, or API knowledge
- AJAX calls automatically to load dynamic content
- Built on the well-known and supported jQuery core
- Lightweight size, 12Kb compressed
- Progressive enhancement
- Accessibility support

We've already discussed some of these features. Let's deeply analyze others.

Use of Nonintrusive Semantic HTML5

I know you are hungry: you need to see some code. Here you have it. jQuery Mobile creates webapps from standard and semantic HTML5, perfectly suitable for search engine optimization (SEO) and web performance optimization (WPO) purposes:

```html
<!DOCTYPE html>
<html>
<head>
        <meta charset="utf-8" />
        <title>My first jQuery Mobile code</title>
        <link rel="stylesheet" href="http://code.jquery.com/mobile/1.0/jquery.mobile-
1.0.min.css" />
        <script src="http://code.jquery.com/jquery-1.6.4.min.js"></script>
        <script type="text/javascript" src="http://code.jquery.com/mobile/1.0/
jquery.mobile-1.0.min.js"></script>
      <meta name="viewport" content="width=device-width, initial-scale=1">
</head>

<body>
<div data-role="page" data-theme="a">
        <div data-role="header">
                <h1>jQuery Mobile</h1>
        </div>
        <div data-role="content">

                <ul data-role="listview" data-inset="true" data-divider-theme="b">
                        <li data-role="list-divider">Summary</li>
                        <li><a href="ch1.html">The Platform</a></li>
                        <li><a href="cap2.html">The Page</a></li>
                        <li><a href="cap3.html">Lists</a></li>
                        <li><a href="cap4.html">Components</a></li>
                </ul>

                <ul data-role="listview" data-inset="true" data-divider-theme="d">
                        <li data-role="list-divider">Links</li>
                        <li><a href="http://www.mobilexweb.com">Mobile Web Blog</a></li>
                        <li><a href="http://www.oreilly.com">O'Reilly Media</a></li>
                </ul>

        </div>
    <div data-role="footer">
        <h4>&copy; 2011 Maximiliano Firtman @firt</h4>
    </div>
</div>
</body>
</html>
```

You can see in Figure 1-6 how this sample renders on many mobile browsers, including non-jQuery Mobile compatible ones, as in Figure 1-7. As you can see, there is no Java-Script code there for initialization or any other stuff. Just some JavaScript includes.

Be patient, we will start analyzing the jQuery code in the following chapters.

Figure 1-6. How our first simple jQuery Mobile code looks on different devices: iOS, webOS, and Android

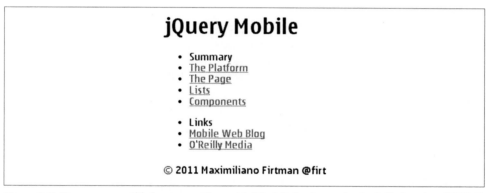

Figure 1-7. On noncompatible browsers, jQuery Mobile falls back to a simple, fully functional HTML file

Progressive Enhancement

Progressive enhancement is a simple but very powerful technique used in web design that defines layers of compatibility that allow any user to access the basic content, services, and functionality of a website, while providing an enhanced experience for browsers with better support of standards. jQuery Mobile is totally built using this technique.

The term *progressive enhancement* was coined by Steven Champeon in 2003 (*http://www.hesketh.com*), and while this approach wasn't defined for the mobile web specifically, it is perfect for mobile web design.

Progressive enhancement has the following core principles:

- Basic content is accessible to all browsers.
- Basic functionality is accessible to all browsers.
- Semantic markup contains all content.
- Enhanced layout is provided by externally linked CSS.
- Enhanced behavior is provided by unobtrusive, externally linked JavaScript.
- End user browser preferences are respected.

This list sounds like jQuery Mobile's feature list, doesn't it? That's right. A jQuery Mobile application will also works on a very basic browser without CSS or JavaScript support. And that is a great feature for a mobile webapp.

Accessibility Support

From Wikipedia:

> Web accessibility refers to the inclusive practice of making websites usable by people of all abilities and disabilities. When sites are correctly designed, developed, and edited, all users can have equal access to information and functionality.

Web accessibility inside mobile browsers has just begun; however, jQuery Mobile is now fully compatible with W3C's WAI-ARIA specification on compatible browsers (*http://www.w3.org/TR/wai-aria/*). At the time of this writing, only iOS 4.0 or higher is compatible with this specification with the feature called VoiceOver.

Therefore, a jQuery Mobile webapp will provide an accessible experience to users with visual disabilities on iPhone, iPod, and iPad.

Testing Webapps

We have already mentioned that a jQuery Mobile webapp will work on almost every modern desktop browser. However, it would be better if we could test them in a more accurate environment (see Figure 1-8).

To test the mobile webapp in different environments, we can use:

- Real devices
- Remote labs
- Emulators
- Simulators
- Lot of friends

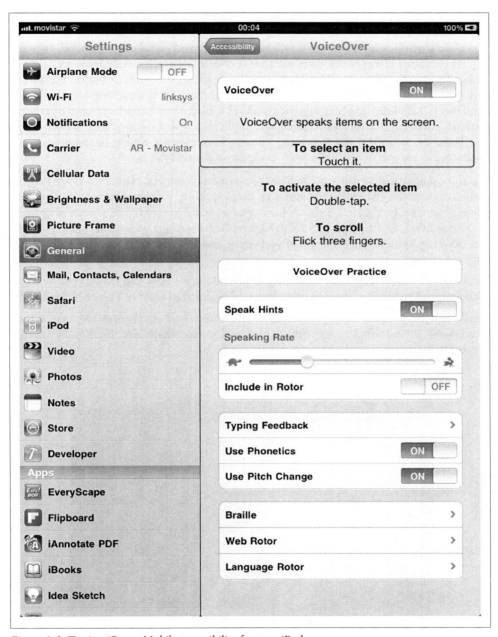

Figure 1-8. Testing jQuery Mobile accessibility from an iPad

Emulators and Simulators

The most useful tools for our work will be emulators and simulators. Generally speaking, an emulator is a piece of software that translates compiled code from an original architecture to the platform where it is running. It allows us to run an operating system and applications on another operating system. In the mobile development world, an emulator is a desktop application that emulates mobile device hardware and operating systems, allowing us to test and debug our applications and see how they are working. The browser, and even the operating system, is not aware that it is running on an emulator, so we can execute the same code as on the real device.

We should also add to our mobile development environment classic tools for project and configuration management, such as bug tracking, version control, and project management tools. Figure 1-8 shows how you can test jQuery Mobile accessibility from an iPhone, iPod, or iPad with iOS 4.0 or higher. Go to Settings → General → Accessibility and activate VoiceOver. Now close your eyes and browse your website using your fingers and ears.

Figure 1-9 shows how an Android Emulator provides a full Android OS on your desktop with images for different devices including tablets, such as Galaxy Tab or Nook Color.

Emulators are created by manufacturers and offered to developers for free, either standalone or bundled with the Software Development Kit (SDK) for native development.

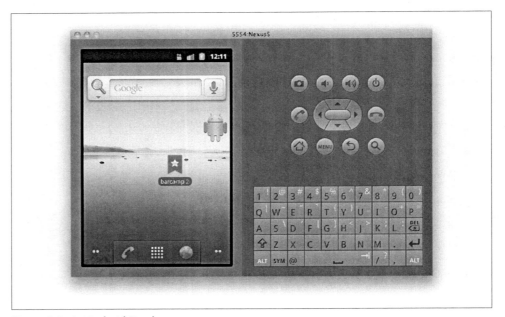

Figure 1-9. An Android Emulator

There are also operating system emulators that don't represent any real device hardware but rather the operating system as a whole. These exist for Windows Mobile and Android.

On the other hand, a simulator is a less complex application that simulates some of the behavior of a device, but does not emulate hardware and does not work over the real operating system. These tools are simpler and less useful than emulators. A simulator may be created by the device manufacturer or by some other company offering a simulation environment for developers. In mobile browsing, there are simulators with pixel-level simulation, and others that neither create a skin over a typical desktop browser (e.g., Firefox or Safari) with real typography nor render engine simulation. Figure 1-10 shows how the iOS Simulator provides you with an iPad for free inside your Mac. The same can happen for other tablets, also with Windows or Linux desktop machines.

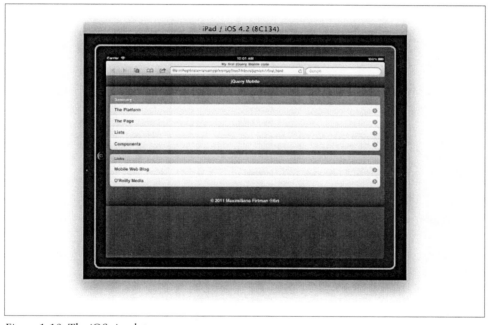

Figure 1-10. The iOS simulator

Even with emulators, the final rendering and performance will not be exactly the same as in the real device. Therefore, real device testing is a good practice, even if we are going to do it only on some key devices.

For mobile web development, we will find emulators from Nokia, Symbian, BlackBerry, Android, webOS, and Windows Mobile and simulators from Apple for the iPhone and iPad (though only for Mac OS X).

Some browser-based emulators (that finally work on many different platforms), like the Opera Mobile emulator, are also available.

Table 1-2 shows the available emulators and simulators for download.

Table 1-2. Available mobile and tablet emulators and simulators for download

Name	Platform	Type	Browsers available	Windows	Mac	Linux
iOS Simulator	iOS	Simulator	Safari	No	Yes	No
Android Emulator	Android	Emulator	Android Browser and downloadable	Yes	Yes	Yes
HP webOS Emulator	webOS	Emulator	webOS Browser	Yes	Yes	Yes
Nokia Symbian Emulators	Symbian	Emulator	Internal Browser and downloadable	Yes	No	No
Windows Phone Emulator	Windows Phone	Emulator	Internet Explorer	Yes	No	No
Nokia Series 40 Emulators	Nokia OS	Emulator	S40, Ovi Browser, Opera Mini	Yes	No	No
BlackBerry Simulators	BlackBerry OS	Emulator	BB Browser, downloadable	Yes	No	No
BlackBerry PlayBook Simulator	Tablet OS	Emulator	Internal Browser	Yes	Yes	Yes
Opera Mobile Emulator	Many	Browser Emulator	Opera Mobile	Yes	Yes	Yes
Opera Mini Simulator	Many	Online Browser Emulator	Opera Mini	Yes	Yes	Yes
PhoneGap Simulator	Many	Simulator	PhoneGap hybrid	Yes	Yes	Yes
Adobe Device Central	Many	Simulator	Many	Yes	Yes	No

An up-to-date list of emulator download URLs can be found at *http://www.mobilexweb .com/emulators*.

Remote Labs

A remote lab is a web service that allows us to use a real device remotely without being physically in the same place. It is a simple but very powerful solution that gives us access to thousands of real devices, connected to real networks all over the world, with a single click. You can think of it as a remote desktop for mobile phones.

The most useful services on the market are the following:

Keynote DeviceAnywhere (commercial)
 http://www.deviceanywhere.com

Perfecto Mobile (commercial)
 http://www.perfectomobile.com

Nokia Remote Device Access for Symbian and MeeGo (free)
 http://www.mobilexweb.com/go/rda

Samsung Lab.Dev for Android (free)
 http://www.mobilexweb.com/go/labdev

For updated information on this topic, go to *http://www.mobilexweb.com/go/labs.*

## CHAPTER 2

Starting with the Framework

Preparing the Document

Let's get our hands dirty and create the typical jQuery Mobile webapp template.

Requirements

Our HTML5 document needs to include:

- The jQuery core JavaScript file
- The jQuery Mobile core JavaScript file
- The jQuery Mobile core CSS file
- The jQuery Mobile theme CSS file (optional)

In addition, jQuery Mobile will use a series of PNG files for some of the UI but we don't need to explicitly link them. There is also a version of the CSS file that includes both the core file and the default theme.

Before coding, our first decision is about resources' hosting. There are two approaches:

- Host all the files within our project
- Use a CDN (Content Delivery Network)

Hosting the Files

If you want to host all the files with your webapp, you need to download the latest ZIP package from *http://jquerymobile.com/download*. The ZIP name will include the version of the framework, for example: *jquery.mobile-1.0.zip*.

The jQuery Mobile package does not include the jQuery core. You need to also download it from *http://jquery.com* (production version is recommended).

In the *jquery.mobile-XX.zip* package, you will find the following structure:

- *demos* folder
- *images* folder
- *jquery.mobile-XX.css*
- *jquery.mobile-XX.js*
- *jquery.mobile-XX.min.css*
- *jquery.mobile-XX.min.js*
- *jquery.mobile.structure-XX.css*
- *jquery.mobile.structure-XX.min.css*

XX will be the version number, including release type, for example: *1.1b1* for *1.1 Beta 1*, *1.0rc2* for *1.0 Release Candidate 2*, or *1.0* for *1.0 final* version.

As we can see inside the package, there are two types of JavaScript/CSS files: one with the *min* suffix and one without it.

The files with the *min* suffix are the recommended version for production, because they are minified (compressed, without spaces, comments and line-breaks). If you need to debug inside jQuery Mobile, you can use the non-suffixed versions.

 jQuery Mobile 1.0 requires jQuery code 1.6.4. Don't try to use a later version of the core because it might be incompatible. If you are using a later version of the mobile framework, check the documentation to verify which core framework version is the one you need to use.

In the most common situation, you will add the following files to your project's root folder:

- *jquery-XX.js* (from the jQuery core)
- *images* folder
- *jquery.mobile-XX_min.js*
- *jquery.mobile-XX_min.css*

If you are creating a webapp using *PhoneGap* or another offline/hybrid mechanism, it's better to embed the files inside your package so the webapp can work offline.

The files with the *structure* name are useful if we are going to create our own theme as we will see later in this book.

jQuery Mobile's License

Usage of jQuery Mobile (and jQuery, the core) is free of charge and they are open source with dual license, MIT or GPL version 2. The MIT license is the recommended choice for most projects and it does not require anything from us. The only important thing to remember is to not delete or change the copyright information at the top of the files. If you have any doubt, you can check *http://jquery.org/license*.

If you host the files on your server, you need to verify that the files are being gzipped on your server if the client supports compression. This will reduce the jQuery Mobile JavaScript and CSS transfer and load time by 80%. If you don't know how, just ask your provider or check in at *http://mobilexweb.com/go/performance*.

Using a CDN

There is a simpler way of using jQuery Mobile: Content Delivery Networks (CDNs). A jQuery CDN is just a public server on the Web hosting the files for us. This approach has its advantages and disadvantages.

The main disadvantage is that our webapp will work only if the public CDN is online. Of course, they are prepared for that and they have all the possible support for being online 24/7. However, some projects need to not rely on third-party servers, such as offline webapps.

 If you are creating hybrid or native apps with jQuery Mobile (such as PhoneGap apps), you should not use a CDN. If the device has lost connection, you could not even show a nice alert using the framework. If you are creating HTML5 offline webapps, you can use the CDN if you add them to the application manifest.

The main advantages of using a CDN are as follows:

- You can use jQuery Mobile now, in one second without downloading anything.
- Your server will deliver fewer files, producing less traffic.
- Your webapp will take advantage of caching: if the user has visited other webapps using jQuery Mobile with the same CDN, her browser may already have all the resources in the cache.
- For most shared hosting servers, jQuery Mobile resources will load faster from a CDN.

- Your webapp will take advantage of the different domain usage for performance purposes.
- On some CDNs, you can link directly to a single location that always features the latest version. However, this is not always recommended, because you will never know how your webapp will respond to newer versions without testing.

There is no room in this book to talk about web performance optimization (WPO) for mobile browsers. If you want to check more about this, go to *http://www.mobilexweb .com/go/performance* and follow Steve Souders's blog at *http://stevesouders.com*.

For the jQuery core, there are several CDNs from which to choose:

- Official jQuery CDN
- Microsoft jQuery CDN (*http://www.asp.net/ajaxlibrary/CDN.ashx*)
- Google AJAX Libraries API (*http://code.google.com/apis/libraries/*)

At the time of this writing, the Official jQuery CDN and Microsoft CDN are hosting the jQuery Mobile files.

Using a CDN is really simple. You just need to copy and paste the URL to the JavaScript or CSS external file, and that's all. In *http://jquerymobile.com/download/*, you will find a copy-and-paste snippet that looks like this:

```
<link rel="stylesheet" href="http://code.jquery.com/mobile/1.0/
jquery.mobile-1.0.min.css" />
<script src="http://code.jquery.com/jquery-1.6.4.min.js"></script>
<script src="http://code.jquery.com/mobile/1.0/jquery.mobile-1.0.min.js"></script>
```

If we are providing our own theme (as we are going to see later), we need to use the following snippet:

```
<link rel="stylesheet"
href="http://code.jquery.com/mobile/1.0/jquery.mobile.structure-1.0.min.css" />
<-- Our theme CSS file here -->

<script src="http://code.jquery.com/jquery-1.6.4.min.js"></script>
<script src="http://code.jquery.com/mobile/1.0/jquery.mobile-1.0.min.js"></script>
```

As you can see, there are just three external resources to a *code.jquery.com* hosting server with minified versions of every resource. You don't need to download anything, including images, CSS, or JavaScript code to use it. Remember to check the latest version available on the website.

Latest builds

If you always want to run your code with the latest version, jQuery CDN offers you new resources to embed in your code. Remember that these versions change automatically, so though your code works today, it may have problems tomorrow. This option should be used for development and testing purposes. Remember that this version may include unstable development code.

The files to include for using the latest builds are these:

```
<link href="http://code.jquery.com/mobile/latest/jquery.mobile.min.css" rel="stylesheet"
    type="text/css" />
<script src="http://code.jquery.com/jquery-1.6.4.min.js"></script>
<script src="http://code.jquery.com/mobile/latest/jquery.mobile.min.js"></script>
```

The advantage of the latest development builds is the ability to use new features not available yet on the latest production build.

Main HTML5 Template

To create a jQuery Mobile webapp, you just need to create an empty HTML5 file. If you have never created an HTML5 document, it's very easy and similar to an HTML 4.01 file.

The *DOCTYPE* (first line in the document) is very simple: `<!DOCTYPE html>`.

And the other change is the `meta charset` tag, inside the `head` tag: `<meta char set="utf-8" />`.

There is no space in this book to talk in detail about changes from HTML 4.01, but just know that these changes are also compatible in some older non-HTML5 compatible devices where jQuery Mobile also works.

 If you use Dreamweaver, starting with the CS5 version, you can create an HTML5 empty template by selecting HTML5 from the Document Type drop-down list in the New Document window. If you don't have this option, you need to first download the 11.0.3 or newer update from the Adobe.com website or the Adobe Updater application.

The official recommendation from the jQuery Mobile team is to include the JavaScript and CSS resources inside the `head` tag (hosted or CDN-based) and add a viewport `meta` tag:

```
<!DOCTYPE html>
<html>

<head>
        <meta charset="utf-8" />
        <title>Your Title</title>
        <link rel="stylesheet"
```

```
        href="http://code.jquery.com/mobile/1.0/jquery.mobile-1.0.min.css" />
    <script src="http://code.jquery.com/jquery-1.6.4.min.js"></script>
    <script type="text/javascript"
     src="http://code.jquery.com/mobile/1.0/jquery.mobile-1.0.min.js"></script>
  <meta name="viewport" content="width=device-width, initial-scale=1">
</head>

 <body>

 </body>

 </html>
```

That is all! We have just created an empty jQuery Mobile document. Of course, the
body is empty and we will revisit that shortly.

The viewport

The viewport is the area in which the page fits. You can specify its width and height,
and it can be larger or smaller than the total visible area of the screen. This is where the
scale and zoom features of the mobile browser come into play. If you are creating a
mobile-friendly website, it shouldn't need to be zoomed in or out or it should start with
a visible area equal to the device's screen width, so you can say to the browser that you
want to start with a scale of 1:1 (viewport area:visible area). Let's take a look at Figure 2-1 to see what's happening to jQuery Mobile on iOS without a viewport
definition.

 jQuery Mobile alpha versions used to create the viewport automatically.
If you are migrating an older jQuery Mobile alpha webapp, remember
that you will need to add the viewport metatag explicitly on your pages.

The typical viewport metatag for jQuery Mobile will look like this:

```
<meta name="viewport" content="width=device-width, initial-scale=1">
```

You can also indicate that you don't want the user to change that scale (with gestures
or buttons):

```
<meta name="viewport" content="width=device-width, initial-scale=1, user-scalable=no">
```

Figure 2-1. In jQuery Mobile we need to define a viewport meta tag to avoid this kind of UI problems when loading our webapp

Performance on JavaScript

Before continuing with our webapp, we need to talk about performance. There is a well-known practice inside WPO claiming that inserting external script tags inside the head is wrong from a performance perspective. That is absolutely true. Just read the excellent book from Steve Souders: *High Performance Web Sites* (O'Reilly).

However, from jQuery Mobile's perspective, moving the two scripts (jQuery and jQuery Mobile) to the end of the HTML file may lead to a non-desired result: your webapp will be shown as plain HTML without CSS for some milliseconds until the framework is downloaded and executed, even if we put the CSS file in the head.

That is because of the progressive enhancement approach that jQuery Mobile uses inside the framework. The CSS file does not do anything on the rendering without the JavaScript.

Therefore, it is better to have them both in the head, even if we have a small performance delay.

Adobe Dreamweaver Support

Starting from version CS5.5, Adobe Dreamweaver has official support of jQuery Mobile inside the tool. You can download a free trial from *http://www.adobe.com/go/dream weaver*.

The first version of Dreamweaver CS5.5 includes jQuery Mobile alpha 3 and not the latest release. Check *http://mobilexweb.com/go/ dwjqm* for instructions on how to update to the latest version. You can always start with alpha 3 and change it manually. Later versions of Dreamweaver will include the latest stable version at the time of release.

The support includes the ability to start a page using jQuery Mobile. To do that, just open Dreamweaver, go to File → New, select *Page from Sample* → Mobile Starters, and you will have the ability to select from three templates (as seen in Figure 2-2):

- jQuery Mobile from CDN
- jQuery Mobile with local files
- jQuery Mobile with local files, including PhoneGap support (to be covered later in this book)

Every template starts with a jQuery Mobile document with four pages linked between one another.

The best part of using Dreamweaver is not the templates, but the code syntax assistant. You can start typing `data-` to receive a list of possible jQuery Mobile `data-*` values. Or you can receive a list of possible values for each `data-*` jQuery Mobile attribute (at least defined up to alpha 3).

With the new multiscreen preview method available in Dreamweaver since CS5.5, you can see how jQuery Mobile adapts itself to different screen sizes and orientations, including smartphones and tablets.

You will also find a new menu under Insert called "jQuery Mobile" that has snippet code for most of the UI components we are covering in this book.

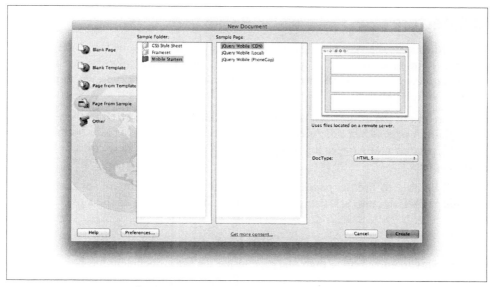

Figure 2-2. Dreamweaver from CS5.5 supports jQuery Mobile templates from scratch.

Previewing Files

To see jQuery Mobile in action inside Dreamweaver you need to use the Live View function, as seen in Figure 2-3.

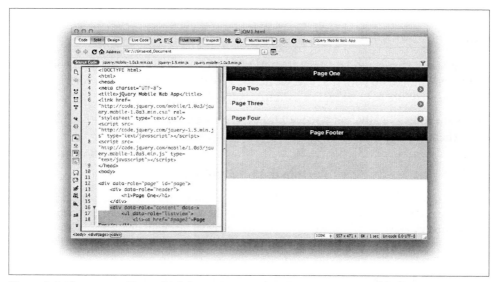

Figure 2-3. You can see jQuery Mobile in action inside Dreamweaver using the Live View

Architecture

jQuery Mobile uses a very simple and powerful approach to define the content of the webapp. Remember that we've already discussed that the framework uses an unobtrusive approach, meaning that our HTML documents will work even without jQuery Mobile loading properly.

The main unit of the framework is the page. Just like normal HTML files then? No. Let me explain. A page is just a `div` element with a specific role. One HTML document can host one page or many pages inside the same file. And that is a new concept for most web designers.

We will be able to link to pages inside the same HTML document, or to pages on external HTML documents, using simple HTML markup, such as the a tag.

Cards Idea

The ability to embed more than one *page* inside the same document has been in the mobile web field for more than 10 years. The now obsolete Wireless Markup Language (WML) standard had the ability to insert many visual pages inside the same document with the goal of reducing latency and download times. jQuery Mobile follows the same idea implemented over normal HTML and JavaScript.

In the WML world, every page was called a *card* and a WML document was called a *deck*. A WML file used the `card` tag for defining a page inside a document, while jQuery Mobile typically uses a `div` tag with a specific role.

Roles

jQuery Mobile uses standard HTML markup, such as the `div` tag. To define what the framework should do with that `div`, we define a *role*. A role in the framework is defined using the attribute `data-role`. For example, `<div data-role="page">`.

The main roles available on jQuery Mobile 1.0 are defined in Table 2-1, and we will cover them throughout the book.

Custom data-* Attributes

The usage of `data-<something>` or `data-*` attributes on an HTML tag is an HTML5 feature called *custom data attributes* (defined in the W3C specification) that allows us to define whatever attribute we want to add to a tag while maintaining an HTML-valid document. It is useful for adding custom metadata to tags without invalidating the markup.

jQuery Mobile often uses this ability to define custom attributes for the framework. But don't get confused: `data-role` is not a new HTML5 new attribute. Its usage is an implicit contract between the framework and us.

The great feature of custom attributes is that they also work on non-HTML5 browsers without any serious issue.

If you are using Adobe Dreamweaver starting from CS5.5 version, you will have automatic jQuery Mobile suggestions when typing `data-` inside an HTML element.

Table 2-1. Main roles available in jQuery Mobile 1.0

Role	Description
page	Defines a *page*, the unit that jQuery Mobile uses to show content
header	Header of a page
content	Content of a page
footer	Footer of a page
navbar	Defines a navigation bar, typically inside a header
button	Renders a visual button
controlgroup	Renders a component
collapsible	Collapsible panel of content inside a page
collapsible-set	Group of collapsible panels (accordion)
fieldcontain	Container for form fields
listview	Content of multiple items as a list
dialog	Dialog page
slider	Visual slider for Boolean values
nojs	Element that will be hidden on jQuery Mobile's compatible browsers

Theming

jQuery Mobile uses a powerful theming mechanism to define visual appearance of the user interface. We are going to cover theming and custom personalization later in this book, but it's important to know now that every UI element (such as a page, button, or component) can use a different color swatch inside a theme.

 The framework up to 1.0 includes only one default theme, and a Theme Roller (an online webapp to create your own theme) is available at *http: //jquerymobile.com/themeroller* to define our own theme without coding CSS files directly.

A theme is a group of definitions for layout, styles, and colors. Every theme includes a set of color swatches that we can change anywhere in our webapp. Color swatches are created to have different options to show elements. A color swatch is defined by a letter, from a to z. The default theme includes swatches from a to e with the ability to add more letters of our own.

Table 2-2 shows the conventions about the color swatches as seen in Figure 2-4.

Table 2-2. Color swatch conventions

Letter	Description	Color in the default theme
a	Highest level of visual priority (default on toolbars)	black
b	Secondary level of visual priority	blue
c	Baseline level (default swatch for most situations)	silver
d	Alternate secondary level	gray
e	Accent	yellow

A color swatch is defined on every jQuery Mobile HTML element with `data-theme` and the letter to assign, for example: `data-theme="e"` for using the accent swatch.

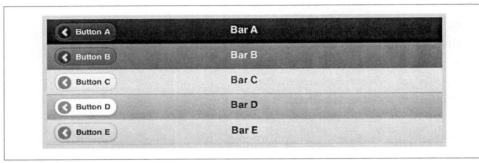

Figure 2-4. Default themes from a to e

Typically we can change the color swatch of lots of elements in our webapp, such as pages, lists, buttons, elements, form elements, and toolbars. We don't need to change them to all the same elements at the same time. We can use color swatches to highlight one element from another.

Color swatches use a cascading system. That means that if a wrapper element defines a swatch color, its children will use that swatch unless a new one is defined explicitly.

The Page

We know that the *page* is the main unit for jQuery. A typical page will be divided in three parts: *header*, *content*, and *footer*. The only mandatory section is the content. Every part is declared using `div` tags with the corresponding role:

```
<div data-role="page">

    <div data-role="header">

    </div>
    <div data-role="content">
```

```
        </div>
        <div data-role="footer">

        </div>

    </div>
```

Every part, including the page, the header, the footer, and the content can have its own swatch color from the current theme.

 The page-role element is not mandatory on a single page document and if we don't provide one, the framework will add one by itself. However, it's a good practice to add it, as it will make our code cleaner and safer for future changes.

In Figure 2-5 we can see a diagram of a typical jQuery Mobile document. Remember that this page needs to be inside an HTML5 document's body with jQuery Mobile embedded.

jQuery Mobile will manage orientation changes itself (portrait or landscape) on most devices, adapting the UI automatically to the new viewport.

 If we want to provide content for non-A-grade compatible browsers, we can add the role nojs, for example <div data-role="nojs">. This content will automatically be hidden for A-grade browsers.

On compatible devices, such as Android-, webOS- and iOS-based ones, jQuery Mobile will try to hide the browser's address bar by manipulating the initial scroll. This is done to render a more native app look and feel. However, this hack will only work if the content is tall enough to fit the available space. If the page does not contain enough content, the address bar will be visible at all times.

The header and the footer

In the header and footer, we can insert whatever HTML we want. However, because of the standard jQuery Mobile stylesheet, the best rendering UI will be achieved using h1 in the header and h4 in the footer. We will see later in this book how to customize the UI.

The footer is optional but the header is generally needed in webapp navigation UI. The header structure is predefined and is divided into three subareas: left, title, and right.

We will cover the left and right areas later. For now, let's say that these are places prepared for action buttons.

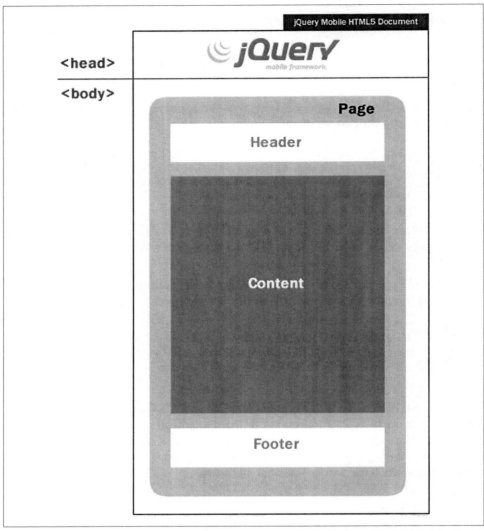

Figure 2-5. A typical page contains a header, a content area, and an optional footer inside a jQuery Mobile document

The title is automatically taken from any hX tag, such as an h1 or h2 element. The space available for the title is limited and it will be automatically cropped if it doesn't fit. On most compatible devices, we will see an ellipsis as in Figure 2-6. This behavior is also replicated in the footer.

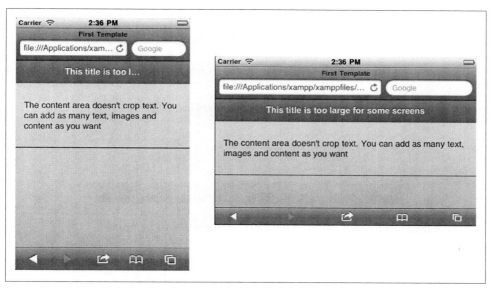

Figure 2-6. If the title doesn't fit, jQuery Mobile adds an ellipsis at the end

The content

The content area can have any HTML code. Typically we are going to use some of the styled controls included with the framework, such as buttons, lists, or forms.

Let's improve our sample, as seen in Figure 2-7:

```
<div data-role="page">

    <div data-role="header">
        <h1>Our first webapp</h1>
    </div>
    <div data-role="content">
        <p>This is the main content of the page</p>
    </div>
    <div data-role="footer">
        <h4>More on mobilexweb.com</h4>
    </div>

</div>
```

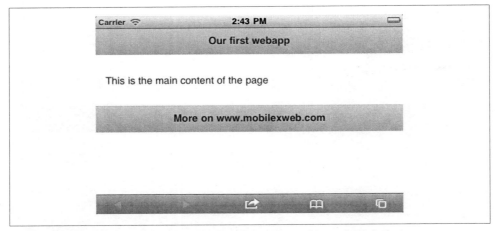

Figure 2-7. Each role (header, content, footer) has a nice iOS-like UI by default

 If you insert code inside a `page`, but outside a `header`, `content`, or `footer` section, jQuery Mobile stylesheets will not work, and you will have some UI bugs if you don't take care of them manually.

Navigation

For navigation between pages, we will use standard a elements. jQuery Mobile will take them and do the magic for us.

First of all, there are different types of hyperlinks that we can make:

- Internal links to another page in the same document (known as a multipage document)
- External links to a page in other jQuery Mobile documents
- Absolute links to non-jQuery Mobile documents
- Mobile special links

Linking between jQuery Mobile's pages (first two cases) creates two special linking behaviors:

- It creates a transition animation between pages, on compatible devices (such as iOS- and Android-based devices).
- If running on a browser (and not in chromeless installed app), the browser's back button will automatically go back to the first page.

A great feature of jQuery Mobile is the detection of the browser's back button to deliver a backward navigation option using techniques transparent to us. Some devices, such as Android- and BlackBerry-based ones, have hardware back buttons that will also work for going back to the previous page.

 In multipage documents, the first page in the DOM will be shown with the first load.

The navigation from the second page to the first one after a back event is fired is done using the same transition effect in reverse.

This back pattern is inspired by iOS and other mobile OS's user interfaces' patterns. jQuery Mobile will stack every new page the user accesses so she can go back anytime to any previously viewed page.

This navigation is entirely done by the framework. jQuery Mobile manipulates the current URL, adding hash values after the initial URL. On some devices, this process can cause a strange effect. While the address bar is hidden, the user navigates to another page, the address bar appears for a second, and then it hides again. This effect only happens with browser-based webapps. You can avoid it by using a full-screen webapp or a hybrid native app, as we are going to see it later in this book.

Back Button

If we want to add a visual "back" button at the left of the header, we can use the `data-add-back-btn="true"` attribute on our page. The button label can be customized using `data-back-btn-text` also applied on the page and the button color swatch can be defined using `data-back-btn-theme`. For example:

```
<div data-role="page" data-add-back-btn="true" data-back-btn-text="Previous"
    data-back-btn-theme="e">

</div>
```

 If you are creating a browser-based experience and not a chromeless webapp (such as an installed webapp), you should know that every browser provides a back button either as a touch button or as a hardware key. Therefore, creating an explicit button for going back will only duplicate actions and use valuable space on the screen. If you are creating an installed chromeless webapp, you should always include an explicit back button.

Internal Page Links

We have already mentioned that a jQuery Mobile document can nest multiple pages inside. To do that, we add multiple pages as body's children. We need to define a id (identification name) using standard HTML for every page, so we can then access them.

To create a link to another page inside the same document, we just need to use #<id> in the href attribute, where <id> is the identification name of the target page. For example: <a href="#next">.

 An external page link must be hosted in the same domain as the current page or hosted in the same package in a native app. If you link to a document in another domain, it will be treated as an absolute external link unless you enable cross-domain AJAX loading from JavaScript.

By default, the framework uses the document's title element as the browser's title. This title is useful for browser-based apps and is shown on top of some browsers as well as when a user bookmarks the page. If we want to update this title when the user accesses a new internal page, we can do it with the data-title optional attribute of every page.

Let's see a sample (shown in Figure 2-8):

```
<body>

<div data-role="page" id="page1">

   <div data-role="header">
      <h1>First page</h1>
   </div>
   <div data-role="content">
      <p>This is the main content of the page.</p>
      <p>You can go to the <a href="#page2">second page</a>.</p>

   </div>
   <div data-role="footer">
      <h4>mobilexweb.com</h4>
   </div>

</div>

<div data-role="page" id="page2" data-title="This is the second page">

   <div data-role="header">
      <h1>Second page</h1>
   </div>
   <div data-role="content">
      <p>This is the main content of the second page</p>
      <p>You can go back using the header's button, <a href="#page1">clicking here</a>
or using your browser's back button.
   </div>
   <div data-role="footer">
```

```
        <h4>mobilexweb.com</h4>
    </div>

</div>

</body>
```

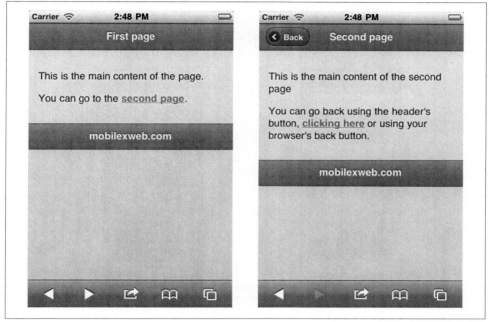

Figure 2-8. Navigation between internal pages is easy and transparent using standard link tags

Can we create a whole webapp using only one HTML document? If we don't require any dynamic content, we can. However, remember that when nesting multiple pages inside a document, the user will need to download the document completely, even if he does not see all pages. We need to find the balance between performance and availability to decide how many pages and which pages should be delivered in the same document.

In Figure 2-9 you can see a diagram of internal page navigation.

We could store some stats from our website to know which pages the user is likely to visit, so we can prefetch them as pages in the same document.

 When the framework finds a link to the previous page, it automatically converts it in a back action link, so you will see a reverse animation, and the action will not add a new entry in the history. If you want a link to go back, you can use `data-rel="back"` on any a element.

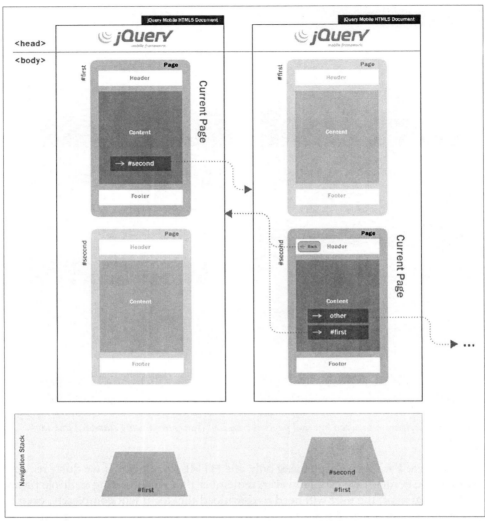

Figure 2-9. When navigating between internal pages, every forward link will add an entry in the navigation stack, while every back action will remove the last entry

External Page Links

If we don't want to include a page inside the same document as the first one, or if we need to dynamically create the content (for example, using PHP or any other server-side code), we can link to another jQuery Mobile HTML document using standard **a** tags:

```
<a href="otherDocument.html">Go to next page</a>
```

That's all? Yes, the framework will automatically trap any link like the one in the previous line and it will provide a very similar experience as the one with internal links.

 An external page link must be hosted in the same domain as the current page or hosted in the same package in a native app. If you link to a document in another domain, it will be treated as an absolute external link.

The only difference is that the framework will be using AJAX to make the request to the other document, will parse its content, add the page included in the current DOM, and make a smooth transition to this new page. While the request is being made, the user will see a nice loading spinner as shown in Figure 2-10. Remember to use `data-title` to update the browser's title after loading the new page.

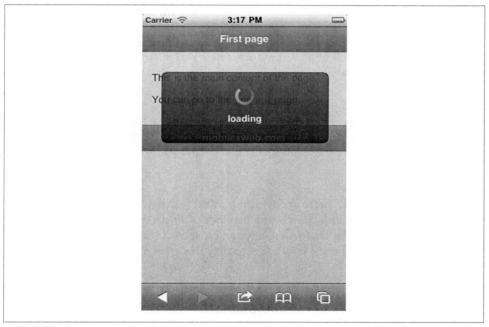

Figure 2-10. When linking to external jQuery Mobile pages, the framework will automatically show an animated spinner while loading the requested page (only if it is taking a long time)

Let's think about it for a second: When jQuery Mobile finds a link on a page, it first detects whether it is an internal link (starting with a hash #) or an external link. If it is an external link without any `rel` or `target` attribute defined (as in the example we've written), it captures the click event creating an AJAX request for the `href` document while showing a progress modal window. When the request has finished, the framework adds the loaded page to the DOM and navigates to it as if it were an internal page.

For browsers not compatible with the framework, external links will work as normal HTML links without any trouble because that is what they are: standard a tags. That is the power of *progressive enhancement*.

jQuery Mobile will automatically add the external loaded page to the DOM with a new ID (defined as the relative URL from the original document), so it will already be "on stage" if the user goes to the same page again while the jQuery Mobile document is still loaded on the browser. This operation is shown on Figure 2-11.

The URL and jQuery Mobile's Navigation

jQuery Mobile uses hash navigation (#<id>) for moving between pages on some devices. Therefore, HTML anchor navigation will not work inside a jQuery Mobile document for scrolling inside the same page.

You need to create JavaScript logic for emulating that feature. In noncompatible devices, internal pages will all display at the same time and internal linking will work as normal HTML anchor navigation links.

There are some mobile browsers supporting History API (one of the new HTML5 APIs) allowing a website to change the entire URL without creating a full-page refresh. jQuery Mobile uses this API on compatible browsers, so instead of hash navigation #<id> for external links, the full target URL will be shown in the URL address bar while the content is still loaded using AJAX from the first document.

An AJAX request can fail. There are several reasons for that, such as a server error, a not-found URL, a connection failure, or a network problem on the device. If the target page cannot be loaded, the user will receive an error alert like the one in Figure 2-12. Later in this book we will learn how to customize this error message.

AJAX or Hijax?

AJAX (originally, Asynchronous JavaScript and XML) is a client-side technique that allows the browser to make a request to the server "behind the scenes" without changing the URL of the page and without blocking the UI while loading. Originally, an AJAX request used XML as the data's format, while now it is more common to transfer JSON-formatted values, or even plain text or HTML.

jQuery Mobile makes AJAX requests between page navigations, requesting the whole target HTML document as plain text for later parsing while still having a normal HTML link in the markup. This pattern is technically known as Hijax and it includes the use of progressive enhancement techniques to make it work.

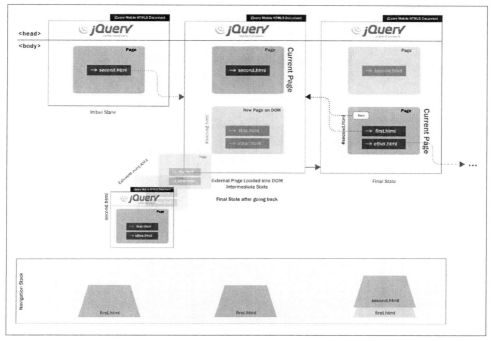

Figure 2-11. The framework will add to the original document's DOM the page loaded via AJAX using an external link so it will be prefetched for future use

To make external page links to a page without any issue, we need to follow these rules:

- The destination must be also a jQuery Mobile document.
- The destination must be hosted in the same domain.
- The destination must be a one-page document.
- If the destination URL is a folder (for example, */clients*), the `href` attribute must end with slash, `href="/clients/"`.
- The `target` attribute should not be declared, as in `target="_blank"`.

 A jQuery Mobile webapp life cycle typically involves one full HTTP request (the first document), many possible internal pages loading, and many possible AJAX requests for external pages. No further HTTP full requests are performed until an absolute external link is found or a B-grade or C-grade browser is in action.

To avoid internal problems with the framework logic, we need to treat external documents with multiple pages as absolute external links, as we are going to discuss in the next section.

Figure 2-12. The message that the user will receive if the destination page could not be loaded in an external jQuery page load

The framework takes from the loaded document only the first page (the first `div` with `role="page"`) and discards any other content. This means that any information you add to the `head` element of the target document will be ignored, with any other content outside the first page element.

With that in mind, any CSS or JavaScript embedded in other documents, as well as the `title` element, will be ignored. Should we remove them? Absolutely not. Remember that jQuery Mobile uses progressive enhancement techniques, so the ignored content will be useful for noncompatible devices loading the full document in the browser. We will talk about how to deal with this limitation later.

Prefetching and Caching Pages

Sometimes we don't want to use external pages because we want to show the next page as soon as the user selects the option. To reduce AJAX times, we can prefetch a page. We can indicate to jQuery Mobile which links should be prefetched by the framework so they can be available sooner on the DOM. To do that, just add the Boolean attribute `data-prefetch` to any link, for example:

```
<a href='newpage.html' data-prefetch>Go to this new page</a>
```

Remember to use this feature only on links with a higher probability of being used. Good usage examples are: paged articles, photo gallery (prefetching the next picture), or a link that statistically we know that most users follow. This feature will add HTTP traffic and consumption to the user, so it should be used with care.

To avoid a large DOM in memory, jQuery Mobile automatically removes from the DOM an external loaded page when it becomes hidden (after going back or going forward to a new page). If the same page needs to be shown again, the framework tries to recover it from a cache; if not, it reloads the page from the server. If we want to force an external page to not be removed from the DOM, we can use the page attribute `data-dom-cache="true"` on the `page` element. Use this feature only if you are sure that the user will return, because increasing the DOM extensively leads to memory and performance issues.

Absolute External Links

Sometimes we want to link to another site or document that does not belong to jQuery Mobile content. For that purpose, we need to explicitly define an absolute external link. We can accomplish this by adding `data-rel="external"` to the a tag.

For example:

```
<a href="http://www.mobilexweb.com" data-rel="external">Check my blog</a>
```

There are other situations where a link is treated as an absolute external one, such as when defining any `target` or when linking to a different domain document, whether or not it's a jQuery Mobile document:

```
<a href="http://www.mobilexweb.com" target="_blank">Check my blog</a>
```

```
<a href="http://www.otherdomain.com/whatever">Check my blog</a>
```

Another way to force a link to be an absolute external one is to use `data-ajax=false` inside the link (useful for pages inside the same domain):

```
<a href="otherpage.html" data-ajax="false">Other page</a>
```

 When the user clicks (or taps with her finger) an absolute link, a jQuery Mobile instance will be unloaded, and the browser will be redirected to the target destination. If we want to maintain our instance while opening the link, we should add `target="_blank"` in the hyperlink. It will work on most smartphones and tablets with multipage navigation support.

If you are creating a native webapp, you should think twice about using absolute external links. By default, the final target will be loaded inside your webapp container (within your application limits), and it may not be what you want. For example, if your native app does not provide any navigation buttons such as back actions, the user will not be able to return to your app. On some solutions, such as PhoneGap, this URL will be opened in the default browser, closing or minimizing your app.

If you link to an absolute external URL within a jQuery Mobile document, it will work as usual but the target page will not have a back button feature. The target page will initiate a new jQuery Mobile instance.

We will cover native development using jQuery Mobile in later chapters, so I leave you to ponder how to solve this problem until then.

Mobile Special Links

Remember we are creating mobile web experiences. We should enhance the user's experience by integrating our app with the device whenever we can. We can include call or send SMS actions using URI schemes. We will get deeper into this ability in "Integrating with the Phone" on page 57.

Remember to always apply progressive enhancement patterns to your website. That means that you should always use standard a links instead of changing pages or navigation using JavaScript. Using standard HTML for navigation will allow your webapp to work on every mobile browser scenario.

Transition Between Pages

As we saw before, when a user goes from a page to another page, jQuery Mobile uses a smooth animation transition. By default, all the transitions are made using a right-to-left animation. This animation pattern is very useful for master detail and general-to-specific navigation. When you get deeper inside the navigation, you see a right-to-left animation. When you go back to previous pages, you see the reverse: left-to-right animation.

Transitions use CSS3, and they are hardware-accelerated on most devices. On some noncompatible devices, there will be no animation between pages.

jQuery Mobile allows us to change or to define explicitly which animation transition we want in every page change. To do that, we need to use the custom attribute data-transition inside the link. Every transition has its reverse counterpart for the back action.

The available transitions (described in Figure 2-13) are:

slide
> The default right-to-left animation.

slideup
> Bottom-to-top animation, mostly used for modal pages.

slidedown
> Top-to-bottom animation.

pop
> The new page will grow from a small point in the middle to a full-screen page.

fade
> A cross-fade animation between old and new pages.

flip
> A 2D or 3D rotation animation. 3D is available only on some devices, such as iOS devices. On other devices, such as those that are Android-based, this transition renders a 2D rotation that may not be the effect you really want.

 Most transition effects inside jQuery Mobile 1.0 were developed by the jQTouch (*http://jqtouch.com*) team, built by David Kaneda and maintained now by Jonathan Stark. Starting with version 1.1, jQuery Mobile is improving the transition effects and adding two new values: flow and turn.

To define a new transition on a link, we apply `data-transition="name"`, for example:

```
<a href="#page2" data-transition="pop">second page</a>
```

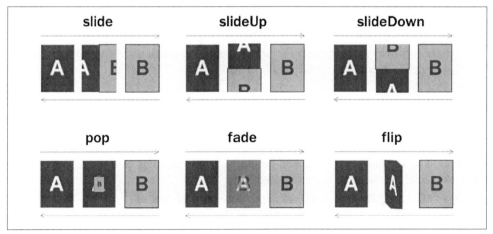

Figure 2-13. These are the possible transitions between pages available in jQuery Mobile 1.0

Transition animations will work only on A-grade browsers with internal and external links to jQuery Mobile pages. Animations will not work with absolute links or with special URI schemes, such as SMS sending.

I recommend you maintain classic transitions between pages and make consistent UI mental patterns. For example, for going deeper in the information or navigation hierarchy, always use the `slide` transition. For lateral actions such as Help, Settings, and Adding new items, you should use any other transition.

Remember that transitions are applied to links, not to pages. This means that the action of going to another page can be done using different transitions if you use many links to get there. Try to maintain consistency in your webapp in these situations.

Reverse Transition

If we want to force a reverse transition (back action), we can specify `data-direc tion="reverse"` on the desired link. jQuery Mobile will automatically make the transition in reverse.

Dialogs

A *dialog* is just another way to show a *page* in our webapp. Therefore, a dialog is not a new thing. It is just a page with a different semantic.

A dialog page is intended for modal messages, lists, or information that does not have any hierarchal relation with the page that links to it.

The main differences between a normal page and a dialog page (shown in Figure 2-14) are:

- It has a *close* action button (with an *X*) at the top left corner where the *back* action button is if we define `data-add-back-btn`.
- A margin conveying to the user that it is not a full-screen page, but a pop-up window that appears over the original page.
- It does not appear on the navigation stack as a new page. (As Figure 2-15 shows, if you open a new page in a dialog, it will open as if the dialog was not there. External loading will also have the same behavior.)

To open a dialog page, we need to use `data-rel="dialog"` inside the `a` tag where the link goes. The `rel` defines the relation between the current page and the linked one (in this case a `dialog` relation). For example:

```
<!-- This link goes to an external page, shown as a dialog -->
<a href="./confirmation.html" data-rel="dialog">Delete this item</a>
```

Figure 2-14. Here you can see the exact same page opened normally and as a dialog

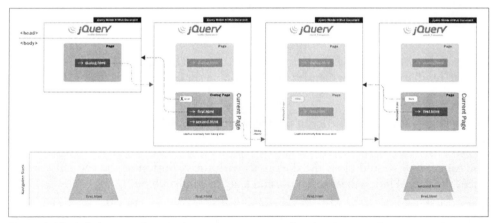

Figure 2-15. A dialog page does not create a new entry in the navigation stack

It is a good idea to change the default transition animation to something other than slide to avoid confusion with the standard animation for pages in the hierarchy. Therefore, a typical dialog-opening link will look like the following code:

```
<!-- This link goes to an external page, shown as a dialog -->
<a href="./confirmation.html" data-rel="dialog" data-transition="pop">
    Delete this item</a>
```

When a page is used as a dialog, we can define the overlay color swatch using `data-overlay-theme`.

 Instead of using `data-role="page"` for a dialog, we can also use `data-role="dialog"` instead of `data-rel="dialog"` on the anchor elements.

Closing or Going Back?

As we saw in Figure 2-14, pages opened as dialogs do not go back, they just close. That means there's a change to the navigation process inside the framework when using dialogs.

The first change is that the dialog "belongs" to the page that opened it. The dialog does not generate a new entry in the history navigation stack.

A dialog page is similar to a pop-up or modal content behavior in typical desktop applications. To close a dialog using a link, button, or other UI control, we should only link to the original page. When jQuery Mobile finds a link to the opener page, it will treat it as a close action.

 In the next chapters, we will analyze how to customize visual design of pages, dialogs, and components using themes and CSS.

Let's suppose we have a delete action on *delete.html*. This link will open a dialog (on *confirm.html*) to let the user confirm the deletion. In the confirmation dialog, we should have two actions: delete and cancel.

Dialog pages do not add entries in the navigation stack. Therefore, if the user reloads the page while the dialog is open, he will get the original page with the dialog closed.

The cancel link should close the dialog, as with the X button at the top-left corner. Then, the cancel link will be just a normal a tag to *confirm.html*.

Just to make our sample a bit nicer, I'm going to jump ahead to the next chapters. Using `data-role="button"` in any link, we will transform the typical underlined link with a nice full-width, finger-height prepared button. In next chapters we will talk more about buttons and how to customize them.

There is a JavaScript way to close a dialog that we are going to see in next chapters. However, using a standard link going back to the opener page is the recommended approach if we are going to target noncompatible devices with our webapp. Remember that jQuery Mobile uses progressive enhancement, and if the browser does not even support JavaScript, the webapp will work anyway

Let's see this in action in Figure 2-16. Here is the code for *delete.html*:

```
<!DOCTYPE html>
<html>

<head>
 <meta charset="utf-8" />
 <title>Up and Running with jQuery Mobile</title>
 <link rel="stylesheet" href="jquery.mobile-1.0.min.css" />
 <script src="jquery-1.6.4.min.js"></script>
 <script type="text/javascript" src="jquery.mobile-1.0.min.js">
 </script>
 <meta name="viewport" content="width=device-width, initial-scale=1">
</head>

<body>

 <div data-role="page" id="main">

   <div data-role="header">
     <h1>Book Properties</h1>
   </div>

   <div data-role="content">
       <h2>Up and Running with jQuery Mobile</h2>
     <p>Author: <b>Maximiliano Firtman</b></p>
     <p>This book has no reviews yet on our database.</p>

       <p>
       <a href="./confirmation.html" data-rel="dialog"
data-transition="pop" data-role="button">
       Delete this book
       </a>

       <a href="" data-role="button">
        Modify this book
       </a>
     </p>
   </div>

   <div data-role="footer">
     <h4>O'Reilly Store</h4>
   </div>

 </div>
```

```
    </body>
  </html>
```

Here is the code for *confirmation.html*:

```
<!DOCTYPE html>
<html>

<head>
 <meta charset="utf-8" />
 <title>Delete Confirmation</title>
 <link rel="stylesheet" href="jquery.mobile-1.0.min.css" />
 <script src="jquery-1.6.4.min.js"></script>
 <script type="text/javascript" src="jquery.mobile-1.0.min.js">
 </script>
 <meta name="viewport" content="width=device-width, initial-scale=1">
</head>

<body>

  <div data-role="page" id="alert">
    <div data-role="header">
      <h1>Confirmation</h1>
    </div>
    <div data-role="content">
      <h2>Are you sure you want to delete this book?</h2>

      <!-- This will be a normal page loading -->
        <a href="delete-yes.html" data-role="button">Yes, delete</a>

      <!-- This is just a close link -->
      <a href="delete.html" data-role="button">Cancel</a>
    </div>

  </div>

  </body>
</html>
```

 If you want to customize the close button text, you can do that on your page using data-close-btn-text.

Opening Pages from Dialogs

Dialogs can have normal links to other pages (or absolute external links). When the user selects a link that points to a different page than the opener (as we saw in the last section), jQuery Mobile will close the dialog, go back to the opener page, and then open the new page as if it were hosted in the opener.

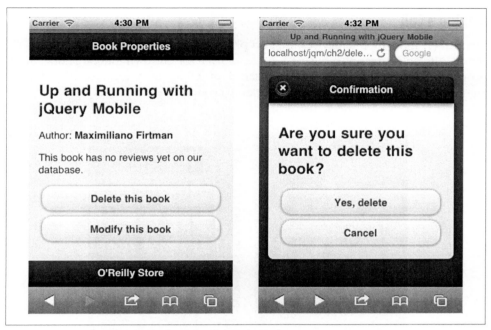

Figure 2-16. Our dialog sample in action on an iPhone

In our sample, if we click on "Yes, delete" the dialog will close and we will see a typical transition to the *delete-yes.html* page.

In Figure 2-15 we can see a diagram of what is happening with the navigation in this situation.

Integrating with the Phone

Repeat with me: "We are designing a page for a mobile device. A mobile device. A mobile device." What does this mean? We should integrate with the phone whenever we can.

One way to do this is through URI schemes, different protocols that we can use inside a `href` of a link `a` tag. I'm pretty sure you are already familiar with the `mailto:` protocol. In mobile browsers, we can find many more. Some of them are compatible with most devices and some others are platform-dependent (for example, iOS). The latest ones are useful if we are creating a native webapp and we are sure in which platform are we running.

Making a Call

Remember: most mobile devices are also phones! So, why not to create link-to-call actions? If you're creating a business guide, or even for our own unique phone, most people will prefer to call a person instead of filling in a form on the device. Figure 2-17 shows how these actions work on a couple of different devices.

Figure 2-17. Palm's webOS and Android show the call window when we activate a tel link

The preferred method (copied from the Japanese i-Mode standards) is to use the `tel:<phone number>` scheme.

```
<a href="tel:+1800229933">Call us free!</a>
```

This URI scheme was proposed as a standard in RFC 5341 (*http://tools.ietf.org/html/ rfc5341*), but be careful reading the specification, because most of the parameters proposed there do not work on any device.

 I recommend inserting the phone number in the international format: the plus sign (+), the country code, the local area code, and the local number. We do not really know where our visitors will be located. If they are in the same country, or even in the same local area, the international format will still work.

If the user activates a call link, she will receive a confirmation alert asking whether to place the call, showing the full number so she can decide. This is to avoid frauds tricking the user into calling another country or a premium number.

Some nonphone mobile devices (such as the iPod Touch or iPad), don't allow voice calls. Instead, they show a prompt to add the phone number to the phonebook (see Figure 2-18).

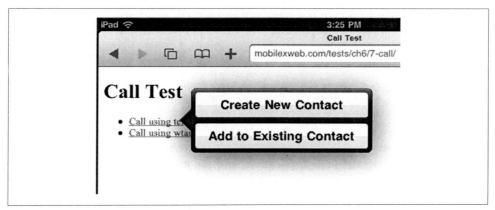

Figure 2-18. Some devices, such as Apple's iPad, don't have calling capabilities but they offer other choices with a tel link

Video and VoIP Calls

iOS-based devices with cameras, such as iPhone 4 and iPod Touch 4G, include a videochat application called FaceTime. If you are targeting these devices, you can create a videocall link using `facetime://<user-name-or-number>`. These links will lead to an error in other devices:

```
<a href="facetime:101010">Call me using Facetime</a>
```

Skype also has its own URI scheme for linking. We need the Skype username for making the link. Optionally, we can also add a `?call` parameter to initiate a call immediately. Without it, we will see the user's profile instead:

```
<a href="skype:skype_user?call">Call us using Skype</a>
```

 If the device does not have the native app to which we are linking, such as FaceTime or Skype, installed, the user will receive an error. It is better to not show those links to noncompatible devices. For device-targeting and content adaptation, check the book *Programming the Mobile Web* (O'Reilly).

Check *http://www.mobilexweb.com/go/uri* for updated information about URI schemes for mobile browsers.

Sending Email

Some modern devices with browsers also have mail applications that can react to the classic web `mailto:` protocol. The syntax is *?parameters*. The detected parameters can change from device to device but generally include `cc`, `bcc`, `subject`, and `body`. The parameters are defined in a URL format (`key=value&key=value`), and the values must be URI-encoded.

Here are some samples:

```
<a href="mailto:info@mobilexweb.com">Mail us</a>
<a href="mailto:info@mobilexweb.com?subject=Contact%20from%20mobile">Mail us</a>
<a href="mailto:info@mobilexweb.com?subject=Contact&body=This%20is%20the%20body">
Mail us</a>
```

Be aware that the `mailto:` mechanism doesn't guarantee that the message will be sent. It generally just opens the mail application, and the user has to confirm the sending after making optional changes. If you need to actually send the mail, use a server mechanism.

Generally, if we want to insert a newline in the body of the email, we can use the carriage return plus line feed characters (%0D%0A). This does not currently work with the Mail application in iOS, but we can insert HTML tags inside the body, so we can use `<br />` for the Mobile Safari browser:

```
<a href="mailto:info@mobilexweb.com?subject=Contact&body=This%20is%20the%20
body%0D%0AThis%20is%20a%20new%20line">Mail us</a>
```

```
<a href="mailto:info@mobilexweb.com?subject=Contact&body=This%20is%20the%20body<br />
This%20is%20a%20new%20line">Mail us from iPhone</a>
```

Sending an SMS

We all like the Short Message Service; that's why mobile browsers generally offer the ability to invoke the new SMS window from a link. To do this, we have two possible URI schemes, `sms://` and `smsto://`. Unfortunately, there is no standard way to know for sure which one is compatible with a user's browser. However, for jQuery Mobile-only smartphones, we can safely use `sms://`.

The syntax is `sms[to]://[<destination number>][?parameters]`. As you can see, the destination number is optional, so you can open the SMS composer from the device without any parameters defined. The parameters involved in defining the body are not compatible with all phones for security reasons (avoid premium SMS texts). As with sending an email, an SMS is not automatically sent when the user presses the link. The link only opens the SMS Composer window; the user must finish the process manually. The destination number should either be an international number or, if it is a short number code, we should guarantee that the user is in the right country and is connected with one of the compatible carriers of that short code.

Here are some samples:

```
<a href="sms://">Send an SMS</a>

<a href="sms://?body=Visit%20the%20best%20site%20at%20http://mobilexweb.com">
Invite a friend by SMS<a>

<a href="sms://+3490322111">Contact us by SMS</a>

<a href="sms://+3490322111?body=Interested%20in%20Product%20AA2">More info for product
AA2</a>
```

Other URI Schemes

If you want to get deeper inside mobile integration from HTML, including MMS, iDEN-networks Direct Call, videocalls, BlackBerry PIN messages, Facebook, Twitter, and other native app integration, check out *Programming the Mobile Web* (O'Reilly).

 Special URI schemes are not a feature of jQuery Mobile. The framework just leaves the URI as-is and the mobile browser becomes responsible for it.

Bringing It All Together

Let's create a simple jQuery Mobile webapp using different URI schemes:

```
<!DOCTYPE html>
<html>

<head>
 <meta charset="utf-8" />
 <title>Up and Running with jQuery Mobile</title>
 <link rel="stylesheet" href="jquery.mobile-1.0.min.css" />
 <script src="jquery-1.6.4.min.js"></script>
 <script type="text/javascript" src="jquery.mobile-1.0.min.js">
 </script>
 <meta name="viewport" content="width=device-width, initial-scale=1">
</head>

<body>

<div data-role="page" id="main">
    <div data-role="header">
      <h1>Special Links</h1>
    </div>
    <div data-role="content">
      <p>Use the following buttons for testing special mobile behaviours.</p>

        <p>
         <a href="tel:+1800229933" data-role="button">
         Call the White House
```

```
        </a>

        <a href="sms:+1800229933" data-role="button">
         SMS the White House
        </a>

        <a href="sms:+1800229933?body=Hello!" data-role="button">
         SMS with a body text
        </a>

        <a href="mailto:info@mobilexweb.com?subject=Sent%20from%20the%20web"
data-role="button">
         Mail me
        </a>

        <a href="skype:maximiliano.firtman?call" data-role="button">
         Skype me
        </a>

        <a href="facetime:+1800229933" data-role="button">
         Call using Facetime
        </a>
         (iOS with camera only)

      </p>
     </div>
     <div data-role="footer">
       <h4>www.mobilexweb.com</h4>
     </div>
    </div>

</body>
</html>
```

## CHAPTER 3

UI Components

jQuery Mobile has a great set of UI components to use on our webapp. Remember that we can always use plain HTML and CSS for adding our own content and ideas. However, for cross compatibility purposes, we are going to give usage priority to framework's components.

We can divide jQuery Mobile's components into the following groups:

- Toolbar components
- Formatting components
- Button components
- List components
- Form components

In this chapter we will examine the first three categories, while saving list and form components for later.

Toolbars

Toolbars are optional areas in our webapp defining headers and/or footers. They are both optional, although headers are usually on every mobile webapp.

We have already talked about the header in the previous chapter: it's the upper bar where the title and/or the back/close button are located. It is defined generally as a `div` with a role or `header` usually with an `h1` title:

```
<div data-role="header">
    <h1>Page's title</h1>
</div>
```

The footer is a similar bar, located at the bottom of the webapp, with a more general purpose. It can include copyright information, a call action link, or a series of buttons such as a toolbar or a tab navigator area. It is usually a `div` with a `footer` role:

```
<div data-role="footer">

</div>
```

Positioning

Positioning toolbars seems easy: headers at the top, footers at the bottom. However, jQuery Mobile's positioning system lets us define different behaviors for both toolbars.

Every toolbar (header or footer) can be positioned in four ways:

- Inline mode
- Standard fixed mode
- Full-screen fixed mode
- True fixed mode

The inline mode is the by-default value for every toolbar. It means the header and footer will flow inline with the page. That means that if the page's content is longer than the available height, the footer will be hidden by default and it will appear after scrolling down, while the header will be visible only while the scroll's position is at the top.

Sometimes it is useful to have the toolbars available at all times and that is why jQuery Mobile offers us the fixed and full-screen modes. To define the positioning mode of a toolbar, we use the attribute `data-position`.

A `fixed` toolbar in jQuery Mobile will be positioned at the top (header) or at the bottom (footer). While the user is scrolling the content of our page, the toolbar will be automatically hidden with a fade transition. When the user finishes the scroll, the fixed toolbar will appear again automatically in the right place at the top or bottom.

If the user taps on some noninteractive content area of the page, the fixed toolbars will convert themselves to inline mode when in fixed mode, and vice versa. This allows the user to move between inline/fixed modes easily by touching the screen and allowing more space for content when needed.

To define a fixed toolbar, as shown in Figure 3-1, we just use `data-position="fixed"`.

A full-screen toolbar is just a hidden fixed toolbar that appears when the user taps on the screen. It disappears again when the user taps on the screen for a second time. The content will take the whole screen, and if the user needs something from the toolbar, he will tap on the content.

With both fixed and full-screen toolbars, the user can show/hide the fixed toolbars with a tap inside the content area. The difference is that with full-screen mode, the toolbars will be really hidden and with fixed mode the toolbars will be positioned inline.

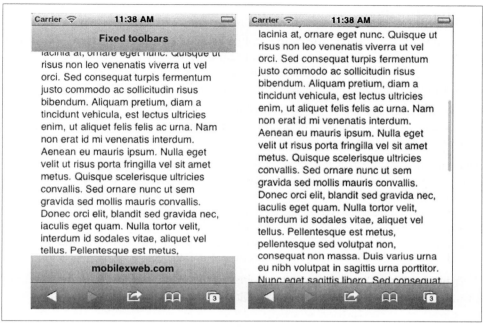

Figure 3-1. A fixed toolbar is at the top (for the header) or at the bottom (for the footer) no matter the content's length or initial scroll value, but while scrolling, the toolbars are hidden

This is particularly useful when showing photos, long text, or large forms so we can take advantage of the whole screen.

When the toolbars are visible, the content will be overlapped. On most browsers, the headers use partial opacity so we can see a transparent background behind the header.

To use this mode, we just define `data-position="fixed"` on the toolbars and then `data-fullscreen="true"` to the page (the element whose `data-role` is `page`).

The following sample defines full-screen toolbars:

```
<div data-role="page" data-fullscreen="true">

    <div data-role="header" data-position="fixed">
     <h1>Page's title</h1>
    </div>

    <div data-role="content">

    </div>

    <div data-role="footer" data-position="fixed">

    </div>

</div>
```

True Fixed Toolbars

At the time of this writing, only some mobile browsers support `position: fixed` and `overflow: auto` in CSS. Fixed position and scrolling zones let us define fixed areas on screen that will be at the same place even if the user scrolls the document. The viewport and zooming in and out usually add complexity to the fixed position idea.

The latest versions of some mobile browsers, including Safari on iOS, Android, Black-Berry, and Nokia's browsers, support `position: fixed` and/or the ability to scroll inside a block with `overflow: auto`.

If we want to provide a true fixed toolbars experience, we can enable the touch overflow ability in jQuery Mobile. Using `overflow: auto`, it will create, with CSS, a smaller scrolling area using than the whole screen so our toolbars will be shown in the same place always. This ability is disabled by default in 1.0, and we can enable it using Java-Script. If we enable this feature, noncompatible browsers will fall back to standard fixed toolbars. Future versions of the framework will obsolete this attribute and they will provide true fixed toolbars by default on compatible devices.

We will cover the jQuery JavaScript API later in this book, but just to understand the idea, to enable true fixed toolbars, this should be the code:

```
$.mobile.touchOverflowEnabled = true;
```

Adding Content to the Header

A standard jQuery Mobile header includes a title, any `hX` child element, and optionally, one or two buttons located at the right and/or at the left of the header. There is also a way to customize the appearance and content as we want.

Adding buttons

Usually (but not always), mobile usability for touch devices uses positive actions to the right and negative actions to the left. Examples of positive actions are Done, Save, Yes, OK, and Send. Negative actions are Cancel, Back, No, Exit, and Log Out.

 Remember from Chapter 2 that we don't need to provide a back action on our own. jQuery Mobile will handle the browser's back button au-tomatically, and we can use `data-add-back-btn="true"` on a page to add a button at the left side of the title. If we are using this option, we should not add any other button to the left.

A header's button is just a hyperlink; it uses an `a` element inside the header. If we provide only one `a` element, it will be located at the left side of the title. If we add two buttons, the first one will be located at the left and the second one at the right of the title.

If we want to force the location of a button, we can use a CSS class for that: `class="ui-btn-right"` or `class="ui-btn-left"`.

The following header will have only one button, as shown in Figure 3-2:

```
<div data-role="header">
  <a href="logout">Log out</a>
  <h1>Title</h1>
</div>
```

Figure 3-2. Headers can contain buttons positioned at the right or left of the title

The following header will show two buttons, the right one using an icon:

```
<div data-role="header">
  <a href="logout">Log out</a>
  <h1>Title</h1>
  <a href="settings" data-icon="gear">Settings</a>
</div>
```

As we can see in the last sample in Figure 3-3, we can apply any of the standard jQuery Mobile icons to a toolbar button using `data-icon` as well as any of the possible values that we saw in the last chapter and covered again in the button sections of this chapter.

Figure 3-3. It's common to use icons inside a toolbar's button to improve user readability.

By default, every toolbar's button inherits the toolbar theme (and if not defined, the page theme). If we want to differentiate one button from the other we can use `data-theme` to change the color swatch appearance of one of the buttons (Figure 3-4).

For example:

```
<div data-role="header">
  <a href="cancel" data-icon="delete">Cancel</a>
  <h1>New record</h1>
  <a href="save" data-icon="check" data-theme="b">Save</a>
</div>
```

Figure 3-4. We can change a button's appearance using a theming color swatch

 If we want to provide our own header's button linked to the previous page, it's important to use `data-rel="back"` on the a element so the framework can handle the back animation and history process correctly.

Adding a logo

It's common to want to show an image/logo instead of text. Use of images in a mobile webapp is beyond the scope of this book, but if you want to show an image in a header using the standard left and right buttons, the best way is to use an `img` tag inside the `h1`:

```
<div data-role="header">
    <a href="cancel" data-icon="delete">Cancel</a>
    <h1><img src="images/logo.png"></h1>
    <a href="save" data-icon="check" data-theme="b">Save</a>
</div>
```

The header will grow to the height of the image automatically, as we can see in Figure 3-5. Remember to match the current color swatch background color. For better compatibility, don't use images larger than 125 pixels.

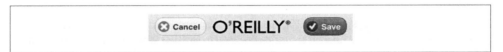

Figure 3-5. Using images for the page's title is as simple as using the img element

 Remember that when using jQuery Mobile, you are targeting different screen sizes and resolutions at the same time, so to include images we'll need some feature detection algorithms to provide the best experience for each device.

Customizing the header

If you don't want the typical jQuery Mobile header rendering, you can deactivate the automatic header behavior (such as `hX` and `a` handling) attaching all your content inside a block container (usually a `div` element).

Customizing the header allows us to add form elements, such as drop-down lists or checkboxes for filtering or menu access. These controls will be discussed in Chapter 5.

Let's see a sample (illustrated in Figure 3-6):

```
<div data-role="header">
    <div>
        <h1>A custom title</h1>
        <a href="#">A non-button link</a>
    </div>
</div>
```

You will need to use your own HTML and CSS code to manage the custom header content. The header's height will grow automatically to match our custom contents.

A custom title

A non-button link

Figure 3-6. We can avoid the automatic behavior of hX and a elements in the headers by using custom headers

Adding Content to the Footer

The footer is far more flexible than the header. As in the header, any a element will be rendered as a button, although there is no left and right button placement in the footer. Every button is added inline, one after the other. It allows us to add as many buttons as we like, as in a button bar.

By default, the framework doesn't add visual padding between the buttons and the footer border, so to provide a better visual appearance, we should add the class ui-bar to the footer.

Let's see a sample (shown at Figure 3-7):

```
<div data-role="footer" class="ui-bar">
    <a href="refresh">Refresh</a>
    <a href="filter">Filter</a>
    <a href="search">Search</a>
    <a href="add" data-theme="b">New Item</a>
</div>
```

Figure 3-7. The footer toolbar is more flexible on the quantity and alignment of buttons than the header

 In the next few pages, we will cover button sets, which allow a series of buttons to be treated as one big group element. We can add this kind of element to the footer.

Footers can also handle form elements and navigation bars, the next topic we are going to cover.

Navigation Bars

A navigation bar (also known as a navbar) is a set of links that can be placed at a toolbar, usually a footer, that combine to create a series of exclusive options. The idea of a navigation bar is to act as a main navigation method for our webapp. On some platforms, such as iOS or Nokia, this navigation bar is also called a tab bar.

 To avoid UI mistakes, you should not use navigation bars for action buttons (such as Save, Cancel, and Search) but as a main navigation structure for your webapp. For action buttons, use normal buttons on a header or footer.

A navigation bar is just a container, usually a `div` element, wrapping an unordered list that includes every action link. The container's role needs to be defined as `navbar`:

```
<div data-role="navbar">
  <ul>
    <li><a href="link1">Option 1</a>
      <!-- ... -->
    <li><a href="linkn">Option n</a>
  </ul>
</div>
```

The navbar's buttons, as seen in Figure 3-8, have a different appearance than the standard buttons we saw in Figure 3-7. The width of the button is calculated as in the following algorithm:

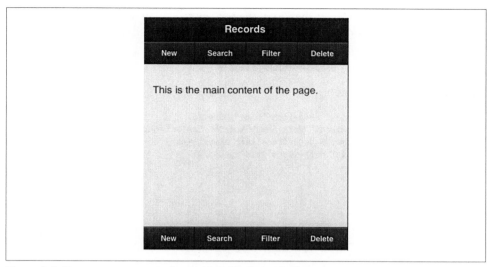

Figure 3-8. Here we can see a navbar inside a header and a footer

- One button on the navbar, 100%
- Two buttons on the navbar, 50%
- Three, four, or five buttons on the navbar, 33%, 25%, or 20% respectively
- Six or more buttons, 50% in multiple lines (two elements per line), as we can see in Figure 3-9

Figure 3-9. If we use more than five buttons, the navbar changes the layout to two buttons per line

 It's a good idea to keep the number of navbar elements below six so they can be rendered in one line. The limit of five is because on most touch smartphones, one-fifth of the screen's width is the maximum preferred width for touch areas.

Using icons

We can use icons for every navbar element, using the standard jQuery Mobile icon mechanism. That is, using `data-icon` with a standard name or even customizing it with our own icons.

By default, the icon is placed at the top of the text, as seen in Figure 3-10. If at least one navbar element uses an icon, the whole navbar height is updated to match the one with the icon:

```
<div data-role="header" data-position="fixed">
  <h1>Home</h1>
  <div data-role="navbar">
    <ul>
      <li><a href="#index" data-icon="home">Home</a>
      <li><a href="#contacts" data-icon="search">Contacts</a>
      <li><a href="#events" data-icon="info">Events</a>
      <li><a href="#news" data-icon="grid">News</a>
    </ul>
  </div>
</div>
```

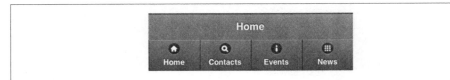

Figure 3-10. Using icons is a good practice for usability and visual appearance.

 With the standard jQuery Mobile methods for creating custom icons, we can use any navbar icons for our elements. There are plenty of free icons available on the Web, with the most popular located at *http:// glyphish.com*.

Selected element

Every navbar can have a selected element, which uses the class `ui-btn-active`. An active element will contrast from the UI based on your current theme (light blue on the default theme). Figure 3-11 shows the selected style for every color swatch.

Figure 3-11. The selected state is clearly shown using a different color swatch

If we are using a navbar as the main navigation for our webapp, it is a good idea to include the Home page as the first element. And it's a good idea to mark the first element as the selected element using `class="ui-btn-active"` on the first `a` element. For example:

```
<div data-role="footer" data-position="fixed">
  <div data-role="navbar">
    <ul>
```

```
      <li><a href="#index" class="ui-btn-active">Home</a>
      <li><a href="#contacts">Contacts</a>
      <li><a href="#events">Events</a>
      <li><a href="#news">News</a>
    </ul>
  </div>
</div>
```

When the user presses on a navbar element, automatically change the selected element to the current selected element. That means that we don't need to be aware of the `ui-btn-active` class update. That also means that we can use JavaScript-based event handlers to manage each element's click and provide changes to the UI and/or page navigation and the navbar selection will be automatically updated.

Persistent Footer

While thinking about navbars, understand that if we change the jQuery Mobile document, a new footer will appear, removing the current one. That means that the selected state, for example, can show some rendering problems (it disappears and appears again or it animates with the page transition). To solve this problem and many others, we can use a persistent footer. When defined, the same footer will persist on the DOM even if we change the page, so the user doesn't see any visual glitch while changing pages.

There is no official way in the framework to define a persistent header. Some hacks to do that include the use of a persistent footer and some CSS tricks to change a footer's position to the top.

To make a persistent toolbar, we need to define a `data-id` identification to a fixed footer for every page where we want to have the same footer. Then, any page that has a footer with the same `data-id` will retain the previous footer without any update.

We also need to use the same footer code and maybe update the selected item. There is one new problem with going forward and back with a navbar and a persistent footer: how to maintain the selected state actively. For that, when using a navbar on a persistent footer we should apply two classes to the selected item: `ui-btn-active` and `ui-state-persist`.

Let's try a full sample with a navbar as a persistent footer and two pages inside the navbar. The results are shown in Figure 3-12.

A persistent footer should be defined as fixed, with `data-position="fixed"`.

```
<!DOCTYPE html>
<html>
<head>
    <!-- Typical jQuery Mobile header goes here -->
</head>

<body>
    <div data-role="page" id="home">

    <div data-role="header">
            <h1>Home</h1>

    </div>

    <div data-role="content">
            <p>This is content for the home</p>
    </div>

    <div data-role="footer" data-id="main" position="fixed">
      <div data-role="navbar">
       <ul>
         <li><a data-icon="home" class="ui-btn-active ui-state-persist">Home</a></li>
         <li><a href="#help" data-icon="alert">Help</a></li>
       </ul>
      </div>
      </div>

    </div>


    <div data-role="page" id="help">

    <div data-role="header">
            <h1>Help</h1>
     </div>

    <div data-role="content">
            <p>This is content for Help</p>
     </div>

    <div data-role="footer" data-id="main"  position="fixed">
      <div data-role="navbar">
       <ul>
         <li><a href="#home" data-icon="home">Home</a></li>
         <li><a data-icon="alert" class="ui-btn-active ui-state-persist">Help</a></li>
       </ul>
      </div>
      </div>

    </div>

</body>
</html>
```

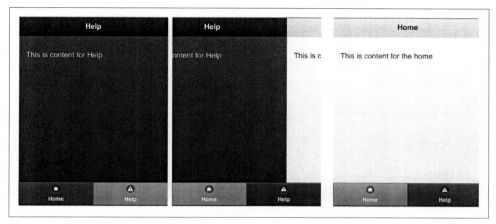

Figure 3-12. Using a persistent footer

Formatting Content

Now it's the time to get deeper into the content area of our webapp. The most important thing to know is that any HTML code will work inside `<div data-role="content">`.

Every theme of jQuery Mobile includes nice styles with padding, margins, sizes, and colors for every standard element optimized for the current theme and mobile device. That includes styles for hX elements, links, bold and emphasized text, citations, lists, and tables.

 If we are going to provide our own CSS styles for the content, we need to be aware of the theming system to avoid UI problems if we change the theme. More about theming and customization later in this book.

Apart from basic HTML elements, there are some components provided by the framework that are defined using `data-role`. In the header and footer, as we saw before, some elements such as hX or a have automatic component rendering behavior. That is not the case with the contents area, except from some form elements, as we are going to see in Chapter 5.

In Figure 3-13 you can see how jQuery Mobile renders some basic HTML elements using the default theme.

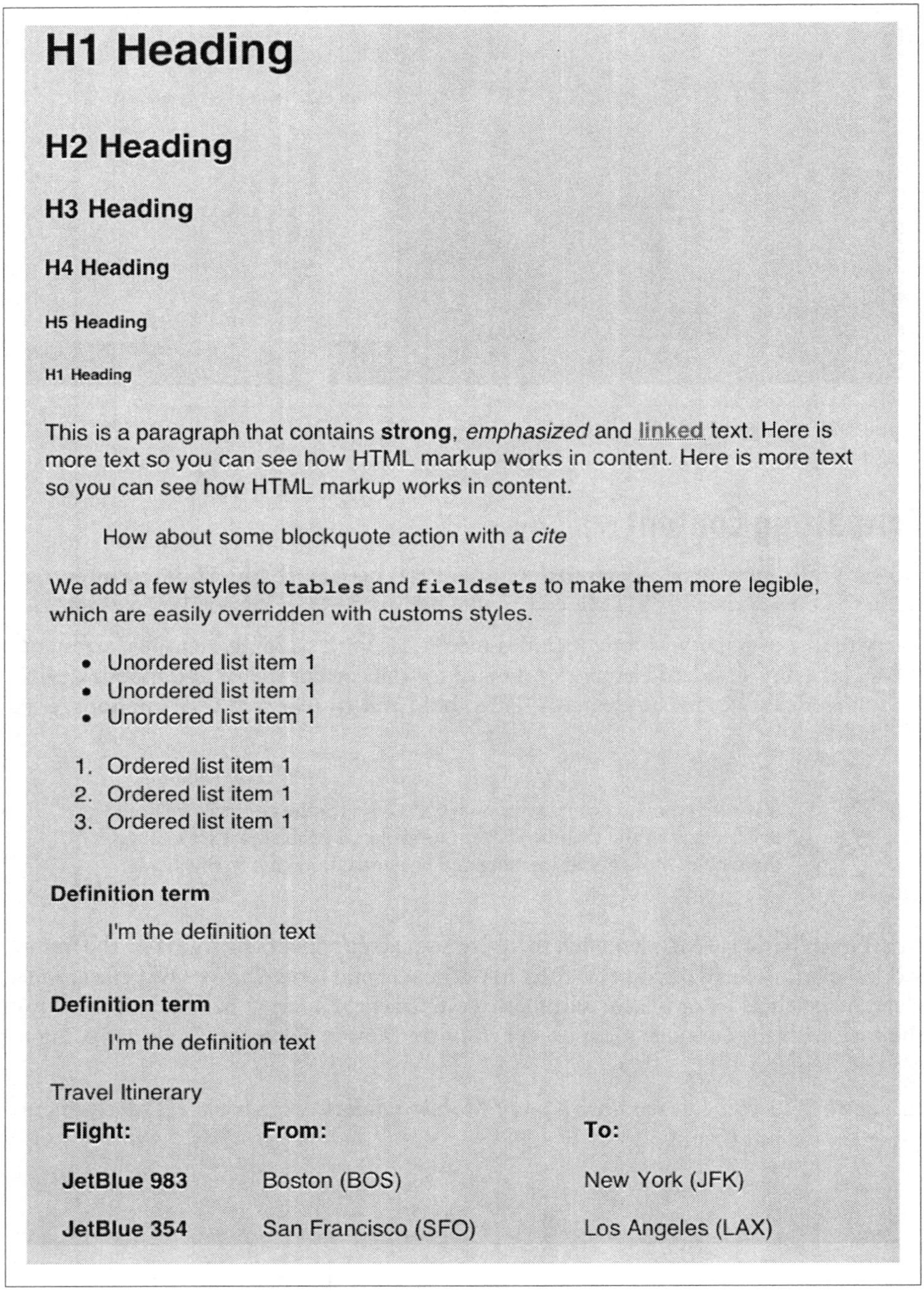

H1 Heading

H2 Heading

H3 Heading

H4 Heading

H5 Heading

H1 Heading

This is a paragraph that contains **strong**, *emphasized* and linked text. Here is more text so you can see how HTML markup works in content. Here is more text so you can see how HTML markup works in content.

> How about some blockquote action with a *cite*

We add a few styles to `tables` and `fieldsets` to make them more legible, which are easily overridden with customs styles.

* Unordered list item 1
* Unordered list item 1
* Unordered list item 1

1. Ordered list item 1
2. Ordered list item 1
3. Ordered list item 1

Definition term

    I'm the definition text

Definition term

    I'm the definition text

Travel Itinerary

Flight:	From:	To:
JetBlue 983	Boston (BOS)	New York (JFK)
JetBlue 354	San Francisco (SFO)	Los Angeles (LAX)

Figure 3-13. Some basic HTML elements rendered using the default theme

Collapsible Content

Remember that we are targeting mobile devices. In mobile devices, space is very limited. That is when collapsible content comes in handy. Collapsible content can be hidden and revealed by a JavaScript behavior after touching a title or button.

jQuery Mobile automatically provides support for this UI design pattern without adding any JavaScript of our own. To create collapsible content, we just need to define a container with `data-role="collapsible"`. This container needs to have an `hX` element that will act as the title to be shown always as the open/close button. The collapsible content will be any HTML code inside that container apart from the title.

By default, jQuery Mobile opens collapsible content when the page loads. We can hide it by default using `data-collapsed="true"` on the container.

Let's see a sample:

```
<div data-role="content">

<div data-role="collapsible">
  <h2>History of Rome</h2>
  <p>There is archaeological evidence of human occupation of the Rome area from at
      least 14,000 years, but the dense layer of much younger debris obscures
      Palaeolithic and Neolithic sites.[11] Evidence of stone tools, pottery and
      stone weapons attest to at least 10,000 years of human presence.
  </p>
</div>

<div data-role="collapsible" data-collapsed="true">
  <h2>Government of Rome</h2>
  <p>Rome constitutes one of Italy's 8,101 communes, and is the largest both in terms
      of land area and population. It is governed by a mayor, currently Gianni Alemanno,
      and a city council.
  </p>
</div>

</div>
```

As we can see in Figure 3-14, jQuery Mobile adds a plus icon and a minus icon for the open and close buttons, respectively. At the time of this writing, there is no way to customize these icons.

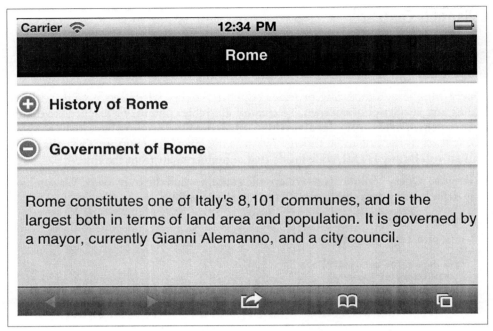

Figure 3-14. Collapsible panels are a good way to show lot of information on the same page, giving the user the ability to close and open details

As with any other rich control, we can change this control's swatch color using `data-theme`. We can also define the additional attribute `data-content-theme` that will affect only the content and not the open/close button of the collapsible panel.

 If you don't define any `hX` element inside the collapsible container, the content will be open and not have any close behavior. If you define more than one `hX` element, the first one will be used as the title and the others will be rendered as content inside.

Nested collapsible contents

You have the option of nesting collapsible content panels. The framework will add an automatic margin to every new level of collapsible panel. It's recommended to not add more than two levels to avoid UI and DOM complexity:

```
<div data-role="content">
  <div data-role="collapsible">
    <h2>Rome</h2>
    <div data-role="collapsible">
      <h3>History</h3>
      <p>There is archaeological evidence of human occupation of the Rome area from
          at least 14,000 years, but the dense layer of much younger debris obscures
          Palaeolithic and Neolithic sites.[11] Evidence of stone tools, pottery and
```

```
              stone weapons attest to at least 10,000 years of human presence. </p>
          </div>
          <div data-role="collapsible" data-collapsed="true">
            <h3>Government</h3>
            <p>Rome constitutes one of Italy's 8,101 communes, and is the largest both in
               terms of land area and population. It is governed by a mayor, currently
               Gianni Alemanno, and a city council. </p>
          </div>
        </div>

        <div data-role="collapsible">
          <h2>Madrid</h2>
          <div data-role="collapsible">
            <h3>History</h3>
            <p>Although the site of modern-day Madrid has been occupied since pre-historic
               times,[23] in the Roman era this territory belonged to the diocese of
               Complutum (present-day Alcalá de Henares).</p>
          </div>
          <div data-role="collapsible" data-collapsed="true">
            <h3>Government</h3>
            <p>The City Council consists of 57 members, one of them being the Mayor,
               currently Alberto Ruiz-Gallardón Jiménez. The Mayor presides over the
               Council.</p>
          </div>
        </div>
      </div>
```

Accordion

There is another typical rich Internet application behavior related to collapsible content: the accordion. This allows you to group collapsible content so that only one panel can be visible at a time. So, when you view one panel, all the others are closed.

jQuery Mobile supports this kind of components as collapsible sets. That is, a container with data-role="collapsible-set" and a group of collapsible panels as children.

If we apply a data-theme or data-content-theme to a collapsible set, every child will inherit these values unless set explicitly.

The template is:

```
<div data-role="collapsible-set">
  <div data-role="collapsible">
      <!-- Collapsible title & content -->
  </div>
  <!-- any collapsible content quantity -->
  <div data-role="collapsible">
      <!-- Collapsible title & content -->
  </div>
</div>
```

By default, jQuery Mobile opens the last collapsible panel in a collapsible set. If you want a different panel to open by default, just use data-collapsed="false" on the element you want to be opened and data-collapsed="true" on all the others.

Let's try a sample:

```
<div data-role="page" id="home">

    <div data-role="header">
        <h1>@firt</h1>
    </div>

    <div data-role="content" data-theme="b">

        <!-- This defines the whole collapsible set (accordion) -->
        <div data-role="collapsible-set">
          <div data-role="collapsible" data-collapsed="false">
                <h2>Books</h2>
            <ul>
                <li>Programming the Mobile Web</li>
                <li>jQuery Mobile: Up & Running</li>
                <li>Mobile HTML5</li>
            </ul>
          </div>
          <div data-role="collapsible" data-collapsed="true">
                <h2>Talks</h2>
            <ul>
                <li>Velocity Conference</li>
                <li>OSCON</li>
                <li>Mobile World Congress</li>
                <li>Google DevFest</li>
            </ul>
          </div>
        </div>
        <!-- end of collapsible set (accordion) -->

    </div>

</div>
```

Figure 3-15 shows a collapsible set with the border styles of every collapsible zone set to have rounded corners.

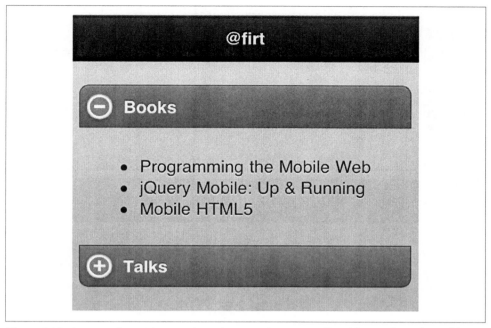

Figure 3-15. An accordion rich control can be created using a collapsible set of panels, visible one panel at a time

Columns

jQuery Mobile offers us some templates to define content to be shown in columns, called layout grids. These grids act like a table without the semantic problem of using table (please, don't use table for anything besides tabular data).

 Remember that you are on a mobile device; columns should be used with care, only to place small elements such as buttons, links, or small items. If you are targeting tablets, you have more space for columns.

The layout grid method uses CSS classes to define grid areas and columns. We can define grids from two up to five columns. Each grid is invisible, uses the whole 100% width, and has no padding or margin defined.

To create a grid, just use a block container, typically a div, with a class of ui-grid-a for two columns, ui-grid-b for three columns, ui-grid-c for four columns and ui-grid-d for five columns. Every grid will divide, by default, the width into equal-width columns.

Every cell should be a block container using `ui-block-<letter>` with `<letter>` being from a to d being the first to the fifth column on the grid.

Let's try a basic two-column example using the HTML5 new element `section`, as we can see in Figure 3-16:

```
<div data-role="content">
  <section class="ui-grid-a">
    <div class="ui-block-a">Column 1</div>
    <div class="ui-block-b">Column 2</div>
  </section>
</div>
```

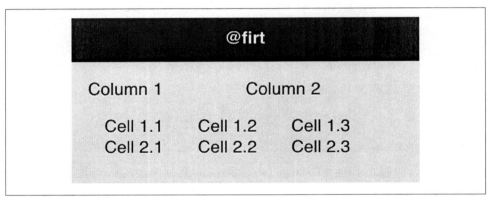

Figure 3-16. We can align elements in up to five equal-sized columns

The layout grids also work as tiled layout. That means, if we add more cells than the available columns, we can emulate different rows using the same grid:

```
<div data-role="content">
  <section class="ui-grid-b">
    <!-- Row 1 -->
    <div class="ui-block-a">Cell 1.1</div>
    <div class="ui-block-b">Cell 1.2</div>
    <div class="ui-block-c">Cell 1.3</div>
    <!-- Row 2 -->
    <div class="ui-block-a">Cell 2.1</div>
    <div class="ui-block-b">Cell 2.2</div>
    <div class="ui-block-c">Cell 2.3</div>
  </section>
</div>
```

Buttons

We've already seen that we can use any a element to make links between pages or to link to external content. However, a typical a element is not rendered easily for touch devices. The element is typically inline, and the clickable area is only the text. That is not a good experience for the touch user. That is why jQuery Mobile provides buttons.

A button is a UI component that feels like...well, a button. That is, a larger clickable area with text and optionally an icon.

A button can be created in different ways:

- Using a `button` element
- Using an `input` element that typically renders a button, including `type="button"`, `type="submit"`, `type="reset"` and `type="image"`
- Any a element with `data-role="button"`

jQuery Mobile's button is typically rendered with a centered label, rounded corners, and shadows, depending on CSS3 compatibility on the browser.

 If we are showing a group of buttons, it's a good UI design pattern to choose one button—the positive and most probable one—to use with a different theme.

The default button uses the whole width of the screen, so every button will use a different line. Let's see a typical sample, rendered in Figure 3-17:

```
<a href="#" data-role="button">Click me!</a>
<button data-theme="b">Click me too!</button>
<input type="button" value="Don't forget about me!">
```

Inline Buttons

We can create inline buttons that don't use the whole width by applying the attribute `data-inline="true"` over the element. Therefore, we can have three buttons in the same row (as seen on Figure 3-17) with the following code:

```
<a href="#" data-role="button" data-inline="true">Button 1</a>
<a href="#" data-role="button" data-inline="true">Button 2</a>
<a href="#" data-role="button" data-inline="true">Button 2</a>
```

 If we want to use inline buttons that take up the whole width of the screen, we can use layout grids to define up to five columns, each one with a button inside.

Grouped Buttons

If we have several buttons that are related to one another, we can group them and receive a different user interface where every button is inside a group container. This technique is called a *grouped control* in jQuery Mobile, and it involves a new component called a control group and a set of buttons.

Figure 3-17. Buttons are the best way to provide interaction in our webapps for touch devices

 When using grouped buttons, don't declare them as inline buttons.

The control group is just a container, typically a `div` element with `data-role="con trolgroup"`. This group will include a set of buttons within it, and the look will be similar to Figure 3-17:

```
<div data-role="controlgroup">
  <a href="#" data-role="button">Button 1</a>
  <a href="#" data-role="button">Button 2</a>
  <a href="#" data-role="button">Button 2</a>
</div>
```

As we can see in Figure 3-18, the buttons are rendered one below the other in a vertical layout. We can create a horizontal layout using `data-type="horizontal"` on the control group as seen in Figure 3-19:

```
<div data-role="controlgroup" data-type="horizontal">
  <a href="#" data-role="button" data-inline="true">Button 1</a>
  <a href="#" data-role="button" data-inline="true">Button 2</a>
  <a href="#" data-role="button" data-inline="true">Button 2</a>
</div>
```

Figure 3-18. When we have different inline buttons, it's better to wrap them in a control group for better appearance

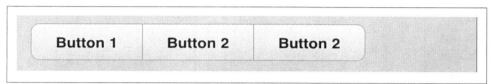

Figure 3-19. If we have fewer than five buttons with short labels, we can use a horizontal control group

 A horizontal group of buttons may look like a selection of different options (pushed buttons). However, up to now they are just buttons grouped together. There is no selected state using this technique. We'll cover group pushed buttons later in this book

Effects

By default, every button is rendered with rounded corners and a shadow. We can change this behavior with Boolean attributes `data-corners` and `data-shadow`. Later in this book we will see how to define this change globally using JavaScript.

So we can create a button without both styles using:

```
<a href="#" data-role="button" data-shadow="false" data-corners="false">Help</a>
```

Icons

jQuery Mobile includes a powerful icon mechanism that allows us to apply themes to buttons as well as many other components where an icon can be used. Therefore, we will talk about icons again later in this book and the options, icon gallery, and functionality will be exactly the same as the analysis we are doing now.

Every button can define an icon through the `data-icon` attribute. This attribute receives an icon name. The name can be one of the gallery (already included with the framework) or a custom name.

The possible icons available in jQuery Mobile 1.0 are described in Table 3-1.

Table 3-1. Icons available in jQuery Mobile

Icon description	Value
Left arrow	arrow-l
Right arrow	arrow-r
Up arrow	arrow-u
Down arrow	arrow-d
Delete (x)	delete
Plus sign	plus
Minus sign	minus
Checkmark	check
Gear icon (settings)	gear
Refresh	refresh
Forward action	forward
Back action	back
Grid	grid
Star	star
Alert (warning icon)	alert
Info (i)	info
Home icon	home
Search icon	search

 Remember that the icon images are provided with the framework, in the download ZIP package or hosted in the CDN. Button icons need the image folder to be available in case we decide to host the framework by ourselves or if we are creating a native app with the framework inside. jQuery Mobile uses CSS Sprites to reduce image loading on icons and it provides two versions: a low and a high DPI version that will be automatically used.

You can see how each icon is rendered in Figure 3-20.

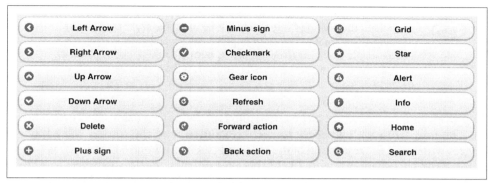

ⓞ Left Arrow	⊖ Minus sign	⊞ Grid
ⓞ Right Arrow	✓ Checkmark	✧ Star
ⓞ Up Arrow	⚙ Gear icon	⚠ Alert
ⓞ Down Arrow	↻ Refresh	ⓘ Info
⊗ Delete	ⓞ Forward action	⌂ Home
⊕ Plus sign	ⓞ Back action	ⓠ Search

Figure 3-20. All the icons included in the jQuery Mobile framework

Creating Custom Icons

If we want to provide our own custom icons, we just need to define our own unique name in the `data-icon` attribute. The preferred naming scheme to use is `<app-name>-<icon-name>`, for example: `myapp-tweet`.

 jQuery Mobile will automatically add a white circled background to the icon, so it will work on every row background without any problem.

jQuery will also expect us to create a CSS class called `ui-icon-<name>`, for example, `ui-icon-myapp-tweet`, and specify a background image. To reduce UI problems, the icon should be in white (or transparent), saved as a 18×18 pixel PNG-8 with alpha transparency. The icon should not have any border; the framework will add it when using the icon in the list view. The icon should also be smaller than 18×18 pixels, because it will be rendered inside a circle that is 18 pixels wide. Our icon should be drawn inside the circle, so don't use the corners.

The class should look like the following code:

```
<style>
  .ui-icon-myapp-tweet {
      background-image: url(icons/tweet.png);
  }
</style>
```

Our custom icon will not work on high-resolution devices, such as iPhone 4 and iPod Touch 4G with retina display. That is because we also must provide a high-resolution version of the icon. To do so, we should provide an alternative CSS selector definition. The image should be exactly double in size, 36×36. We can provide the same image for both low- and high-resolution versions; however, for better results, two images is the recommended solution.

If the CSS style will be applied only on one HTML5 jQuery Mobile document, the preferred way to add it is by using the `style` tag, instead of using an external reference to improve performance. Of course, it's not as simple as I tried to synthesize it, but try to think about performance when adding new external resources, unless you have an active cache policy.

To provide different versions, just use two different definitions using CSS3 media queries. The first definition will apply to every resolution, and the second will apply on devices with twice the resolution of the standard (such as iPhone 4 or newer). We need to force the background size to 18×18, because on these devices `px` refers to virtual points matching two real pixels per virtual point. The class now looks like this:

```
<style>
  .ui-icon-myapp-tweet {
      background-image: url(icons/tweet.png);
  }

  @media only screen and (-webkit-min-device-pixel-ratio: 2) {
    .ui-icon-myapp-tweet {
        background-image: url(icons-hd/tweet.png) !important;
          background-size: 18px 18px;
    }
  }

</style>
```

Let's see how a standard button compares to a custom button (Figure 3-21). The custom app is using the CSS styles we've just defined:

```
<a href="#" data-role="button" data-icon="gear">Help</a>
<a href="#" data-role="button" data-icon="myapp-tweet">Tweet</a>
```

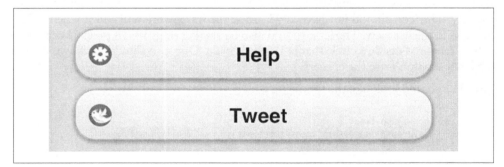

Figure 3-21. We can provide custom icons for buttons and other UI components

Icon Positioning

By default, every icon is rendered to the left of the button's text. We can change its position using the `data-iconpos` attribute, which supports `right`, `left` (default value), bottom, and top. When using bottom or top, the button's height grows. This is particularly useful when used on navigation bars or horizontal grouped buttons.

Let's see different icon positions over the same link (Figure 3-22):

```
<a href="#" data-role="button" data-icon="help" data-iconpos="right">Help</a>
<a href="#" data-role="button" data-icon="help" data-iconpos="left">Help</a>

<div data-role="controlgroup">
  <a href="#" data-role="button" data-icon="help" data-iconpos="bottom">Help</a>
  <a href="#" data-role="button" data-icon="help" data-iconpos="top">Help</a>
</div>
```

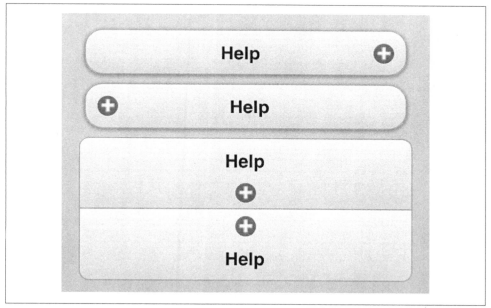

Figure 3-22. With data-iconpos, we can align an icon at any of the four areas shown in this image

Icon-Only Buttons

jQuery Mobile also supports buttons without text inside. This is not the most usable feature because the buttons are too small for touch interfaces. To create an icon-only button, just use data-iconpos="notext" on the button.

Icon Shadow

jQuery Mobile includes an attribute with which you can remove the shadow effect on the icons. For this effect, we can use data-iconshadow="false" on any button element.

## CHAPTER 4

Lists

Up to now, we have created very simple pages rendered by jQuery Mobile. The next big step is to use rich controls and views provided by the framework; in this case, *lists*. Almost every mobile project will have at least one list in its content, so that is why we are going to address this first.

It's difficult to start this chapter with a definition. You already know what a list is. And there is nothing new I can say about them as a general term. Inside jQuery Mobile world, a list is just an ordered (ol HTML element) or unordered (ul HTML element) list inside a page with at least one list item (li HTML element) and the role defined as listview using the HTML5 syntax data-role="listview".

If you want to just show a bulleted or numbered list, you can always render typical ul and ol HTML elements; just remember to not assign any JQM role.

Lists are a powerful solution for many uses inside the framework, as we are going to see in next pages.

The most typical list is an unordered one (ul) that simply exists inside a page without other content. Let's see a simple sample, illustrated in Figure 4-1:

```
<!DOCTYPE html>
<html>

<head>
 <meta charset="utf-8" />
 <title>Up and Running with jQuery Mobile</title>
 <link rel="stylesheet" href="jquery.mobile-1.0.min.css" />
 <script src="jquery-1.6.4.min.js"></script>
 <script type="text/javascript" src="jquery.mobile-1.0.min.js">
 </script>
 <meta name="viewport" content="width=device-width, initial-scale=1">
</head>

<body>

 <div data-role="page" id="main">
```

```
<div data-role="header">
    <h1>HTML5 and APIs</h1>
</div>

<div data-role="content">
    <ul data-role="listview">
        <li>Offline Access
        <li>Geolocation API
        <li>Canvas
        <li>Offline Storage
        <li>New semantic tags
    </ul>
</div>

</div>

</body>
</html>
```

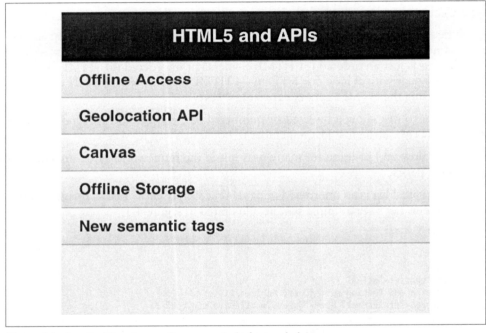

Figure 4-1. A typical list view renders rows nicely for touch devices

jQuery Mobile renders lists optimized for touch usage, as you can see in the default row height used by the framework. Every list item automatically fits the whole width of the page, a typical UI pattern for touch mobile devices. (If we have a long list, we can use fixed toolbars.)

Remember that jQuery Mobile works on the client side. The document with the list can be generated dynamically with any server-side platform, such as PHP, Java, ASP.NET, or Ruby without any issue.

We can also use ordered lists with the ol element. However, if we don't define interactive rows with links, there will not be any rendering difference from ul, as we can see in Figure 4-2:

```
<!DOCTYPE html>
<html>

<head>
  <!-- Typical jQuery Mobile header goes here -->
</head>

<body>

 <div data-role="page" id="main">

   <div data-role="header">
     <h1>Chapters</h1>
   </div>

   <div data-role="content">
      <ol data-role="listview">
          <li>The Mobile Jungle
          <li>Mobile Browsing
          <li>Architecture and Design
          <li>Setting up your environment
          <li>Markups and Standards
          <li>Coding Markup
          <li>CSS for Mobile Browsers
          <li>JavaScript Mobile
          <li>Ajax, RIA and HTML5
          <li>Server-Side Browser Detection
          <li>Geolocation and Maps
          <li>Widgets and Offline webapps
          <li>Testing, Debugging and Performance
          <li>Distribution and Social Web 2.0
      </ol>
   </div>

 </div>

 </body>
</html>
```

This sample shows how jQuery Mobile renders list rows. If the text doesn't fit on a single line, the framework will automatically resize that row.

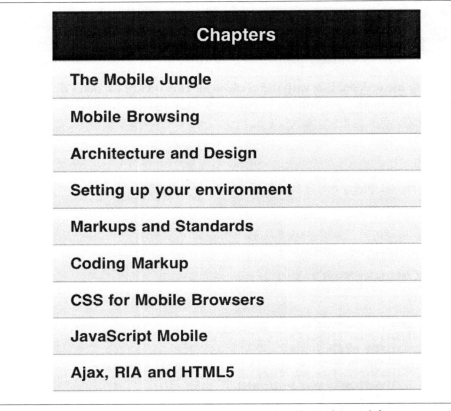

Chapters
The Mobile Jungle
Mobile Browsing
Architecture and Design
Setting up your environment
Markups and Standards
Coding Markup
CSS for Mobile Browsers
JavaScript Mobile
Ajax, RIA and HTML5

Figure 4-2. An ordered list is rendered the same as an unordered list, unless we define an interactive list

 HTML5 does not use XML syntax; therefore it's not necessary to close all tags, like the element li. Of course, you can close them if you feel more comfortable (for example, if you are a developer like me; a non-closing li hurts my eyes).

Full-Page Lists Versus Inset Lists

By default, lists are in a full-page mode. That means that the list covers the whole page contents, as in Figures 4-1 and 4-2. However, on some projects, it can be useful to have lists mixed up with other HTML content. For that purpose, jQuery Mobile offers inline lists. To define them, just add data-inset="true" to the ul or ol elements:

```
<ol data-role="listview" data-inset="true">
    <!-- item rows -->
</ol>
```

In Figure 4-3 we can see how our previous samples are rendered using the inline attribute. As we can see, the table has a slightly different design, with more padding sharing space with other content inside the same page. It also adds nice rounded corners and other CSS3 effects.

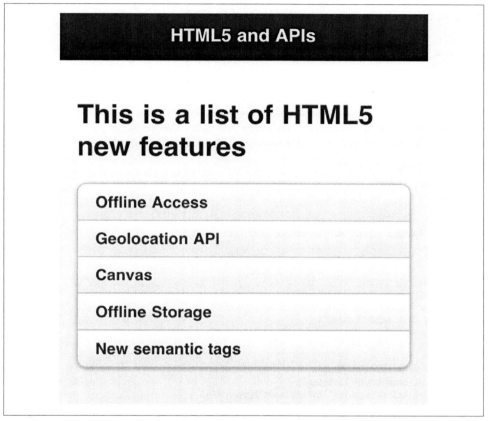

Figure 4-3. An inset table has a very different UI and it can share the page with other content, including other lists

 With lists, we can define color swatches via `data-theme` on the `ul` element and also on every `li` element.

With inline lists we can also design a page with multiple tables inside with optional HTML content between them.

Visual Separators

You can use separators to divide a single list into row groupings with their own titles, as shown in Figure 4-4. It's a common pattern on mobile operating systems, such as iOS on iPhone and iPad. To do this in jQuery Mobile, we can just use a new role available for `li` elements: `data-role="list-divider"`.

 Note that list dividers are just standard `li` elements with a different role, and they are at the same level as the normal row on the DOM tree.

We can divide the list elements into groups using this technique, such as A-Z groups if we are listing alphabetical ordered data or any other classification we want to make. Remember we can change the color swatch to highlight each divider.

Let's run a simple example:

```html
<!DOCTYPE html>
<html>

<head>
  <!-- Typical jQuery Mobile header goes here -->
</head>

<body>

 <div data-role="page" id="main">

   <div data-role="header">
     <h1>World Cup</h1>
   </div>

   <div data-role="content">
     <ul data-role="listview">
         <li data-role="list-divider">Group A
         <li>Argentina
         <li>Nigeria
         <li>England
         <li>Japan
         <li data-role="list-divider">Group B
         <li>United States
         <li>Mexico
         <li>Korea
         <li>Greece
         <li data-role="list-divider">Group C
         <li>Germany
         <li>Finland
         <li>Chile
         <li>South Africa
     </ul>
   </div>
 </div>
```

```
    </div>

  </body>
</html>
```

Figure 4-4. *Here we can see how the row separators render on the list*

 If we are populating the list from client-side code, as in JavaScript, we must call a refresh method after doing so, so the framework can take changes and render them properly. We will cover these techniques later, but for now, if you have only one list on a page with `id page1`, the jQuery code will look like `$("#page1 ul").listview("refresh")`.

In Figure 4-4, we can see how list dividers work over lists.

Interactive Rows

Lists become more powerful when we combine them with touch interaction.

If a list element contains an a element, it will convert that row in an interactive one for touch and/or cursor navigation. One great feature of jQuery Mobile is that the whole row will be interactive automatically for touch no matter where the link is placed inside the row. Meaning the user doesn't need to tap only in the link's text area. She can tap on any pixel in the row.

 An interactive row has a different height than a read-only one. This different design is optimized for touch interaction, as the touch area needs to be large enough to avoid errors. The row text also has a larger font size. In iOS-based devices, 44 pixels is the recommended height for most common controls. Other touch devices use similar sizes.

The framework automatically adds a nice arrow at the right side of the row giving the user a hint that the row is touchable, as seen in Figure 4-5. This icon can be changed using data-icon, as we will see in a minute.

On the same list, we can mix interactive rows with read-only rows. However, the most typical UI design is to have full-interactive or full-read-only lists.

In the following sample, shown in Figure 4-5, we can see interactive rows in action:

```
<!DOCTYPE html>
<html>

<head>
  <!-- Typical jQuery Mobile header goes here -->
</head>

<body>

 <div data-role="page" id="main">

   <div data-role="header">
     <h1>Interactive</h1>
   </div>

   <div data-role="content">
     <ul data-role="listview">
        <li><a href="#page2">Internal Page link</a>
        <li><a href="other.html">External Page link</a>
        <li><a href="http://www.mobilexweb.com">Absolute external link</a>

        <li><a href="tel:+13051010200">Call to a phone number using a link</a>
        <li><a href="javascript:alert('Hi!')">JavaScript link</a>
     </ul>
   </div>
```

```
        </div>

      </body>
    </html>
```

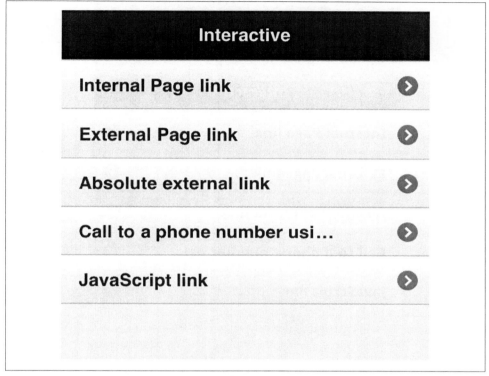

Figure 4-5. Interactive rows are just hyperlinks inside list elements that automatically are clickable and touchable

As we can see in Figure 4-5, when we are working with interactive rows, jQuery Mobile tries to maintain rows of the same height. Therefore, when the row's title doesn't fit in one line, like the fourth row's title, jQuery Mobile will crop the text, adding an ellipsis at the end on CSS3-compatible devices. Keep the length of a row's text to a minimum if you don't have a detail page with the full text.

The a element must be inside the li tag, and there is no obligation to insert the row title as the content of the link. We can just leave the link empty and it will work anyway:

```
<li><a href="#page2"> Internal Page link </a>
```

On some devices with cursor or focus navigation, such as BlackBerry or Android, the user may choose to navigate with the keyboard keys or a trackball. Firing a row (using some OK key or pressing the trackball) will fire the link inside the list element. In

Figure 4-6, you can see how this works on Android devices with a border focus shown typically in orange by the browser on the selected row.

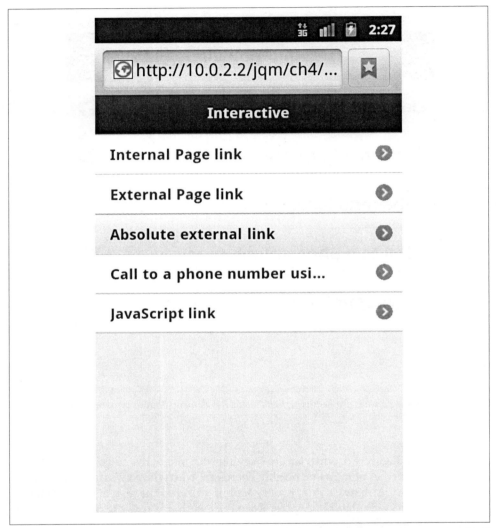

Figure 4-6. On focus-based browsers, interactive lists can be browsed using cursor keys or a trackball

Using interactive lists is the preferred way to create links in a page, instead of using just a tags alone, because they are optimized for touch and cursor-based navigation.

When the user taps an interactive row that generates a page redirection action inside the framework, the row becomes selected while the new page is being transitioned or loaded from the network. A selected row has a different color scheme, as seen in Figure 4-7.

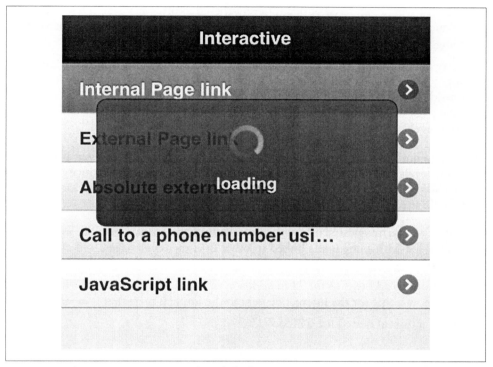

Figure 4-7. When a interactive row is selected, the framework changes its color scheme to a highlight background, light-blue on the default theme

We can change the default interactive row's icon using `data-icon` on the `li` element, for example:

```
<li data-icon="info"><a href="#moreinfo">More information</a></li>
```

If we want to remove the icon on an interactive row, we can use the special `false` value on `data-icon`:

```
<li data-icon="false"><a href="#page2">No icon interactive row</a></li>
```

Nested Lists

Nested lists are a great feature of jQuery Mobile. If you have any hierarchical structure or navigation that you want to show in different pages, as in continents → countries → cities, you can use a nested list.

A nested list is just a list view (a list with the role specified) inside an item of another list view. For example, we can use a `ul` inside an `li` of another `ul`. jQuery Mobile will generate an implicit page for every nested list as if it were created by us explicitly and will make the link between levels automatically.

A nested list will be rendered with a different theme to provide visual reference that it is a second-level list. Of course, we can define theming explicitly with `data-theme` as we are going to see later.

Then, we have different levels of navigation automatically creating only one page. After loading, jQuery Mobile will show only items from the first level, and every item with a list inside it will become an interactive row. If the user selects that row, a transition to a new page will execute showing the next level list view with the back action to the previous level.

There is no limit in the quantity of levels a nested list can have. However, if you have too many levels and items, it's a good idea to use different pages to reduce DOM and initial loading. Nested lists are only recommended for specific situations. Don't create your whole site as a nested list.

Of course, we can mix nested lists with normal interactive rows. Therefore we can have a first level list with some items linked to other documents or pages, and other items with nested lists.

It's important to add text to the `li` in addition to the `ul` or `ol` because the framework needs to show a title for the interactive item in the implicit page that is created.

Therefore, a typical nested list will look like:

```
<li>
    Item title
    <ul data-role="listview">
        <!-- Nested list items -->
    </ul>
```

Let's create a sample, as shown in Figure 4-8:

```
<!DOCTYPE html>
<html>

<head>
  <!-- Typical jQuery Mobile header goes here -->
</head>

<body>

 <div data-role="page" id="main">

   <div data-role="header">
     <h1>Training</h1>
   </div>

   <div data-role="content">
      <ul data-role="listview">
          <li><a href="order.html">Order Now!</a>
```

```
<li>Cities available
    <ul data-role="listview">
        <li>Boston
        <li>New York
        <li>Miami
        <li>San Francisco
        <li>San Jose
    </ul>

<li>Topics
    <ul data-role="listview">
        <li>Intro to Mobile Web
            <ul data-role="listview">
                <li>WML and other oldies
                <li>XHTML MP
                <li>HTML 4.01
                <li>HTML5
            </ul>
        <li>Mobile Browsers
            <ul data-role="listview">
                <li>Safari for iOS
                <li>Android Browser
                <li>Firefox for Mobile
                <li>Opera
            </ul>
        <li>Tablet Browsers
        <li>Using jQuery
    </ul>

<li>Promotions
    <ul data-role="listview">
        <li>10% off before May
        <li><a href="promo3x2.html">3x2</a>
        <li>10% off to subscribers
    </ul>

    </ul>
  </div>

  </div>

  </body>
</html>
```

 In nested tables, jQuery Mobile will automatically use the row text as the title for the newly generated page, so be aware that you need to keep your text as simple and short as possible to fit in the title area.

In Figure 4-8 we can see all the navigation and pages that we get when using a nested list without special effort.

Figure 4-8. Nested lists offer navigation similar to having different pages without creating new pages

 With some jQuery Mobile hacks, we can create links to the automatically generated pages in a nested list manipulating the URL hash. However, if we need to do so, it might be better to have an explicit page created instead of a nested list.

Split Button Lists

Sometimes it's useful if we can have two possible interactive actions active on the same row. The most common scenario is to have a detail action and also an edit action.

For example, if we list contact names on a table, we can offer two possible actions: view details and edit. For that purpose, jQuery Mobile uses what it is called a *split row*. If a list item, li, has two hyperlinks (a element), it will be automatically treated as an split row.

As we can see in Figure 4-9, the row is split in two parts: left and right. The first link in the DOM will be used as the first action, active in the left side of the row. The second link will be used as the alternate action, activated on the right side of the row.

The second link action doesn't need any text inside the link. In fact, the first link action doesn't either. We can leave the a link without contents, and it will be applied to the whole row.

 Following iOS user interface guidelines, the first action should be used for details and the second action should be used for edit. However, that is not an obligation.

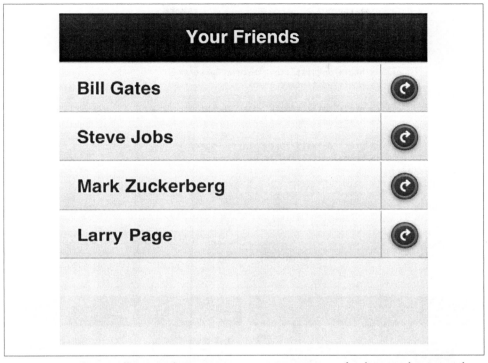

Figure 4-9. A split row allow us to have two active zones per row, one for the typical action and one defined by a separate icon at the right

By default, jQuery Mobile will use a bordered arrow icon for the right button (the second action) a little different than the one for standard interactive rows.

If we want to define a different theme for the right split icon, we can do it using `data-split-theme` over the `ul` tag.

Let's take a look at a sample, shown in Figure 4-10:

```
<!DOCTYPE html>
<html>

<head>
  <!-- Typical jQuery Mobile header goes here -->
</head>

<body>

  <div data-role="page" id="main">

    <div data-role="header">
      <h1>Your Friends</h1>
    </div>
```

```
<div data-role="content">
    <ul data-role="listview">
        <li><a href="details/bill">Bill Gates</a>
            <a href="edit/bill"></a>

        <li><a href="details/steve">Steve Jobs</a>
            <a href="edit/steve"></a>

        <li><a href="details/mark">Mark Zuckerberg</a>
            <a href="edit/mark"></a>

        <li><a href="details/larry">Larry Page</a>
            <a href="edit/larry"></a>
    </ul>
</div>

</div>


</body>
</html>
```

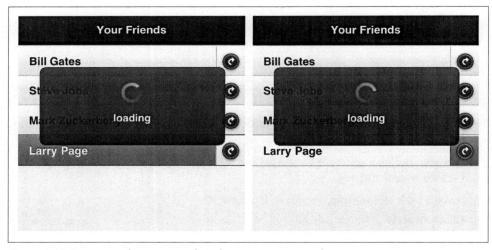

Figure 4-10. Every zone has its own selected state, as we can see here

We can change the icon for the second action using the modifier `data-split-icon`—applied to the list itself (`ul` or `ol` element) and not to the list item (`li` element).

The list view uses the same icon set as for buttons (as we are going to see in the next chapters), but with the addition of a rounded border for a visual difference from normal buttons.

The possible icons we can use up to jQuery Mobile 1.0 are shown in Table 3-1.

We can provide our own icon set using only one image and applying CSS Sprites, like the ones included in the framework.

Managing row importance

If we want some or all rows to be more important than typical ones, we can insert the row's title inside any hx tag, such as h2 or h3. When we do that, that row will grow in height.

If we want a row to be less important (maybe for a not-so-frequent action), we should enclose the row's title in a p tag to reduce the row's height.

In later chapters we will see how to customize list views and rows in a more precise way.

Ordered Interactive Lists

Previously in this chapter, we talked about using ol for defining our list views instead of ul. We've also realized that using ol on read-only lists has no effect on the rendering. That is definitely different when we have interactive rows.

First, one important requirement: all the rows must be interactive for this list to work. Then, we can use ol and our links will be numbered automatically, as we can see in Figure 4-11.

Using Images

In each row we can define one image to graphically identify the item. There are two different kinds of images we can add to every row: icons and thumbnails.

Row Icons

A row icon is an image shown at the left side of the row's title. Don't confuse the row icon with the right arrow on interactive rows or with the split rows's icon.

An icon is a 16×16-pixel image inside the li element, with the class ui-li-icon defined. For example:

```
<li>
    <img src="/icons/email.png" class="ul-li-icon">
    Send by e-mail
```

Icons are usually used for action lists, for example, for a list showing multiple actions we can do with a record (delete, edit, share by email, share in a social network, etc.).

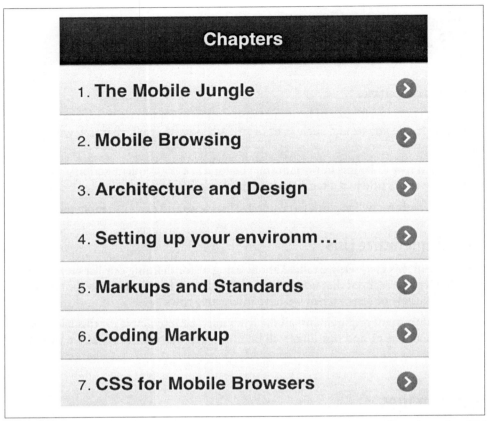

Figure 4-11. If we define a listview role in a ol element with interactive rows, we'll get this ordered UI

Thumbnails

A thumbnail is an 80×80-pixel image that is also positioned at the left of the text. They are preferred to icons when we are showing photos, pictures, or other graphical information attached to each item.

Thumbnails are usually used for lists showing database records, such as friends, books, DVDs, cities, etc.

A thumbnail is defined as an image inside the list item. It doesn't need any special `class` defined:

```
<li>
    <img src="/thumb/washington.png">
    George Washington
```

Let's see icons and thumbnails in action in two inset lists at Figure 4-12.

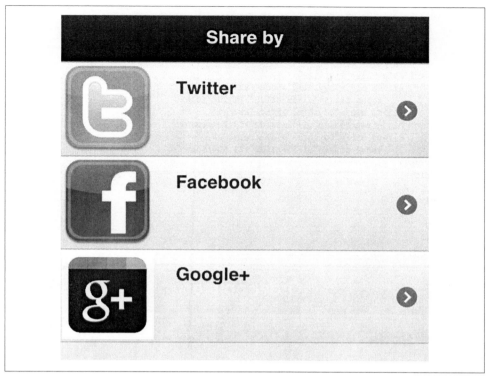

Figure 4-12. A picture worth millions; that is why we can add icons and thumbnails to every list row

Aside Content

Up to now, every list we've designed has only one column for text content. We can add a thumbnail or an icon but only one text column. We can add a second-level column to every row for supplemental information we want to show.

To do so, we can use any HTML element with a class of `ui-li-aside`, such as a `span` or `div` element.

Let's create a sample showing a price as the aside content (Figure 4-13):

```
<!DOCTYPE html>
<html>

<head>
  <!-- Typical jQuery Mobile header goes here -->

</head>

<body>
```

```
<div data-role="header">
  <h1>Order online</h1>
</div>

<div data-role="content">
  <ul data-role="listview">
    <li><a href="buy.html">Soda</a>
        <span class="ui-li-aside">$1.00</span>
    <li><a href="buy.html">Sandwich</a>
        <span class="ui-li-aside">$3.20</span>
    <li><a href="buy.html">Ice cream</a>
        <span class="ui-li-aside">$1.50</span>
  </ul>
</div>

</div>

</body>
</html>
```

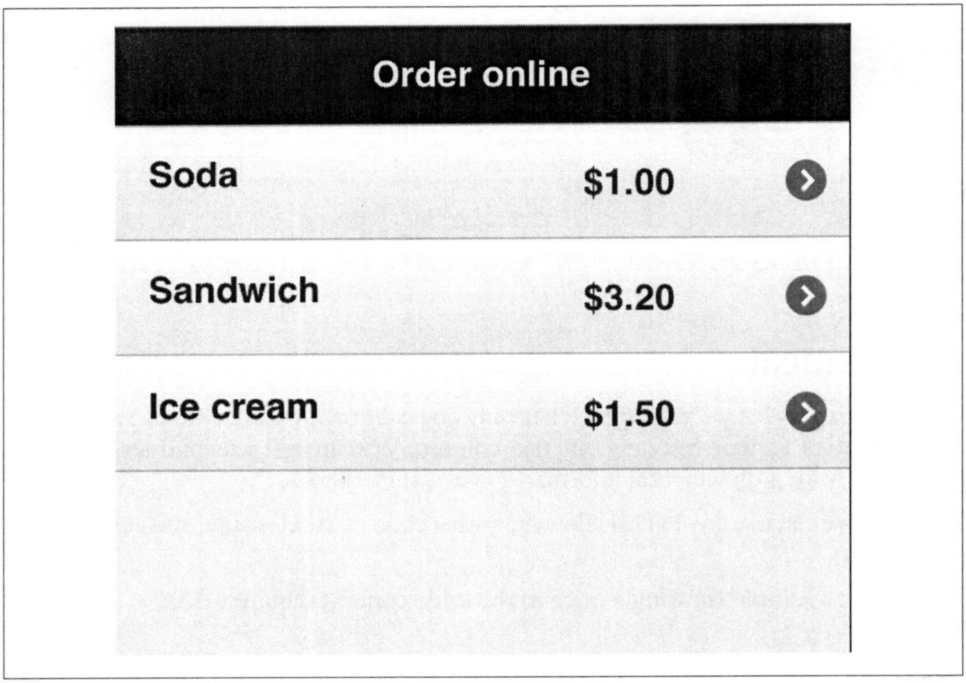

Figure 4-13. With aside content, we can show more information about a row without using a new page

Title and Description

If we want to show both a title and a description as part of the row, we can do it by using some header element hx tag for the title and a p element for the description text. This is not rendered as a second column but as shown in Figure 4-14.

Of course, you can mix title and description with aside content and with icons or thumbnails in the same row.

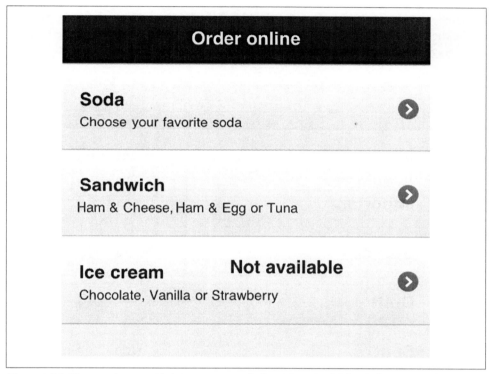

Figure 4-14. If we need to provide long content aside from the title, the best solution is to show a title and a description instead of aside content.

Using Count Bubbles

A count bubble is a circle with a number inside rendered at the right of the row usually showing how many items are in there on interactive rows. It can be used to show unread elements, unfinished tasks, or any other numeric information in a very simple way.

There is no limitation to a numeric value for the count bubble. However, using text is discouraged because the space available is optimized for numeric values. For text, use aside content or description.

Just use any element, such as a `span` tag, with a class of `ui-li-count` inside a list row and that's all. For example:

```
<li><a href="inbox.html">Inbox</a>
    <span class="ui-li-count">86</span>
```

In Figure 4-15 we can see how a count bubble is rendered on an interactive list. We can define the count bubble's color swatch via `data-count-theme` on the `ul` element so we can change the default white background color.

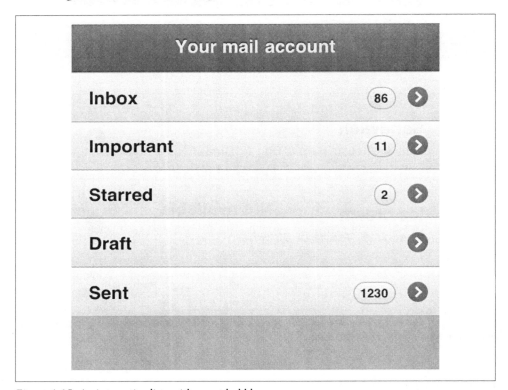

Figure 4-15. An interactive lists with count bubbles

Filtering Data with Search

I've left the best part for the last. Leave your book for a moment. If you are reading this book in any digital format, leave the reader or your browser. Go and take any of the list view samples we've done in this chapter.

Search for the ul or ol element and add `data-filter="true"`, test it and then go back to the book.

The magic of jQuery Mobile has happened. When adding this simple attribute, a search box will be attached automatically at the top the list (full page or inset) and it works!

This feature will filter our list elements based on the user's typing. The search text box looks very nice (as you can see in Figure 4-16), with a search icon at the left side, a watermark hint text, rounded corners, and a clear button at the right side.

Again, for this to work, just use the following code. Please go now to this book's website to grab the source code to copy and paste. Typing it will be very hard for you:

```
<ul data-role="listview" data-filter="true">
  <!-- list rows -->
</ul>
```

We can customize the placeholder text using `data-filter-placeholder`, for example:

```
<ul data-role="listview" data-filter="true" data-filter-placeholder=
    "Search contacts...">
  <!-- list rows -->
</ul>
```

If we want to customize the search bar's color swatch, we can use the `data-filter-theme` attribute.

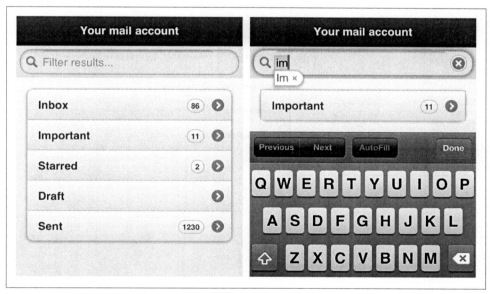

Figure 4-16. Search filters are a magic solution that adds a filtering system without any code

List Views Cheat Sheet

We've covered many features of list views in the last few pages. In Figure 4-17 you will find a quick cheat sheet to understand how to render your list views using HTML markup.

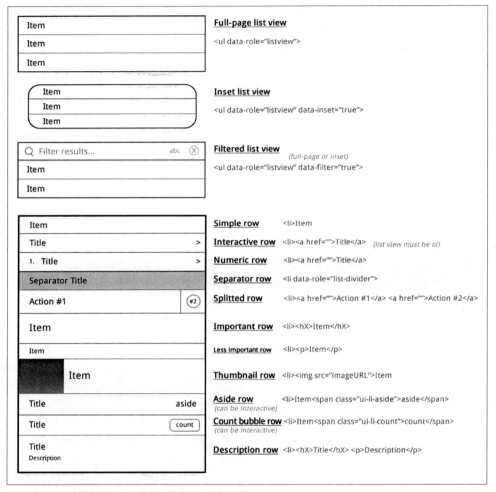

Figure 4-17. All the list view possibilities in one diagram

## CHAPTER 5

Form Components

The jQuery Mobile framework supports standard web forms with automatic AJAX handling on compatible devices and with touch-optimized rendering for standard form controls. That's the first good news about form controls.

When I say standard web form I'm talking about a group of form controls—such as `input`, `textarea`, and `select` elements—inside a `form` element with an `action` attribute defined as the URL that will receive the form's data.

Form Action

Any form action will be handled as we expect. That is, the form will be submitted when the user presses a submit button or when the user presses the Enter key. Did I say Enter key on a mobile device?

We are going to target different devices with different input handling. Some of them will have physical keyboards (maybe with an Enter key); some others will only have a virtual onscreen keyboard. Devices with a virtual keyboards usually have a "send," "submit," or similar button on the keyboard that acts as the submit button while the user is entering form data.

When the form is submitted, jQuery Mobile will use an AJAX transition to the submission page similar to a link to an external page, unless the form is submitted to another domain. The form can use `get` or `post` defined in the `action` attribute of the `form` element.

A typical jQuery Mobile form will look very similar to a typical web form:

```
<form action="send.php" action="get">

</form>
```

A jQuery Mobile form needs a jQuery Mobile document on the results page, similar to an external link. That is because, by default, jQuery Mobile will try to send the form via AJAX using the framework.

The results page will be added to the history's browser if we are using a `get` method using the location hash.

The same `data-transition` and `data-direction` attributes that we saw in Chapter 2 are applicable to `form` elements. Therefore we can define a form submission action to be shown with a pop transition:

```
<form action="send.php" action="get" data-transition="pop">

</form>
```

Forcing a Non-AJAX Form

If we want to force a standard HTTP request without AJAX, we can use `data-ajax="false"` on the `form` element. This is particularly useful if the action is on a different domain host or when using file uploads (more on this later).

Another way to force a non-AJAX submit is by using `target="_blank"` on the `form` element.

 It's possible to define an `autofocus` Boolean value on an input form control to receive focus after the page loads. However, on a jQuery Mobile document, this attribute will work only on the first page and not on newly loaded pages using jQuery Mobile's transitions.

Form Elements

jQuery Mobile supports standard web form controls and new rich controls on the same form. The framework has a feature called "auto-initialization" that takes every web form control and replaces it with a touch-friendly rich control.

The framework also takes new HTML5 input types to a new level, supporting them even on browsers without official support.

The following elements will be rendered as rich controls:

- Buttons, using `button` and `input` elements
- Text inputs, using `input` and `textarea` elements
- Checkbox and radio buttons using `input` elements
- Menus using `select` and `option` elements
- Sliders using `input type="range"` new control
- Slider switches using `select` and `option` elements with a new role

If we don't want jQuery Mobile to render a form control as a rich UI component, we can force it using `data-role="none"` on every form element.

Every form element will use one line and will not share a row with another form control. This is the best solution for user experience on mobile forms. We can always force columns, but it's not recommended for mobile forms.

 When using AJAX, all the pages will share the same DOM, including the webform controls. That is why we need to maintain our form element's unique IDs in our entire site. If we have two forms, don't use the same ID for similar form controls

Labels

A very important element of every form's control is the label. We should always include a `label` element pointing to the right control using the `for` attribute. Let's see an example:

```
<label for="company">Company Name:</label>
<input type="text" id="company">
```

The most important thing to know about labels is that if the user clicks on a label, the form control will gain focus and the user will be ready to use it. Therefore the clickable area of an element is the control itself, plus the label created, a good experience for touch devices.

 If, for any reason, you want a form element without a label, you still need to think in terms of accessibility. That is why you should always have a label and, if you want to hide it, you can apply the class `ui-hidden-accessible` to it or any other HTML element.

Field Containers

A field container is an optional label/component wrapper that enhances the experience on wider screens, such as tablet devices. This container is any block element with `data-role="fieldcontainer"`.

This container aligns the label and form controls correctly and adds a thin border to act as a field separator. The second important feature of a container is that the layout is automatically defined based on the device's width. That is: if the device has a narrow width, the label is placed at the top of the form control; if not, the label is placed at the left in a two-column layout, as seen in Figure 5-1.

We can add a field container to every label/control pair as shown in the following sample:

```
<div data-role="fieldcontainer">
<label for="company">Company Name:</label>
<input type="text" id="company" name="company">
</div>
<div data-role="fieldcontainer">
```

```
<label for="email">Email:</label>
<input type="email" id="email" name="email">
</div>
```

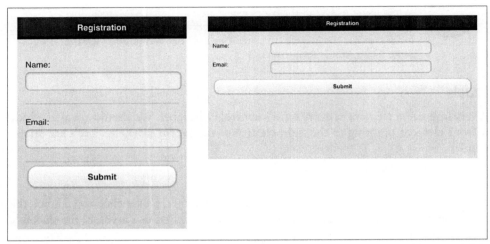

Figure 5-1. The label placement changes from smartphone to tablet based on well-known mobile design patterns

Text Fields

jQuery Mobile supports the basic HTML5 text input controls and renders them according to the current theme and color swatch. These are the available input text fields:

- `<input type="text">`
- `<input type="password">`
- `<input type="email">`
- `<input type="tel">`
- `<input type="url">`
- `<input type="search">`
- `<input type="number">`
- `<textarea>`

When we use any of the previous elements, we will receive a jQuery Mobile control automatically. Remember we don't need to explicitly specify any `data-role`.

 Every input element with the types `button`, `submit`, `clear`, and `image` will be automatic rendered as jQuery Mobile buttons.

If you are thinking: "I only know about `text` and `password` input types," don't worry. `email`, `tel`, `url`, `search`, and `number` are new input types in the HTML5 specification that are very important in the mobile world. As you know, most touch devices don't have physical keyboards. When we define one of these new input types, we will get a different and optimized virtual keyboard as you can see in Figure 5-2.

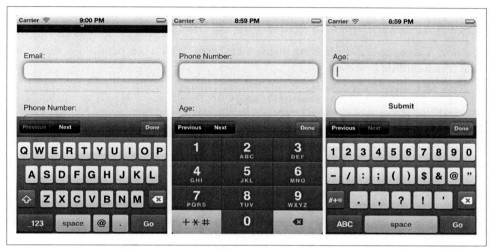

Figure 5-2. Using new HTML5 text input types we can get different virtual keyboards on some mobile devices

 Don't worry about older devices not supporting HTML5 new input types. Every browser will fall back to a basic text field if it doesn't understand the `type` attribute.

The `search` input type has two differences when compared to the typical `text` input type: it has a different UI inside jQuery Mobile and it provides a different "return" key in the virtual keyboard of some devices, as you can see in Figure 5-3:

```
<div data-role="fieldcontainer">
<label for="search">Search:</label>
<input type="search" id="search" name="search">
</div>
```

Auto-Growing Text Area

When we use `textarea` for multiline text input, we will get a complimentary service: auto-growing. jQuery Mobile starts with a two-line height until we enter text that creates a third line. Then, the framework will automatically expand the text area to fit the

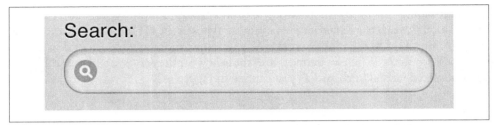

Figure 5-3. A search text input has a different appearance inside a jQuery Mobile document

new line. This is to allow scrolling inside a `textarea`, which is a painful operation on most touch mobile browsers.

```
<div data-role="fieldcontainer">
<label for="comments">Your comments:</label>
<textarea id="comments" name="comments"></textarea>
</div>
```

In Figure 5-4 we can see the auto-growing text area in action.

Figure 5-4. jQuery Mobile automatically expands text areas when the text uses more lines than available

Secure or Not Secure

The usage of the password text input (`<input type="password" />`) on mobile devices is a subject of much debate. The password text input (with the classic stars or circles displayed instead of the typed characters) was originally created because of the possibility of a password or other sensitive data being stolen by someone standing behind the user with a view of the screen. In the mobile ecosystem, the situation is different. With the limited screen size and font size, it is very difficult for another person to see what a user is typing on his mobile phone. Furthermore, typing on non-QWERTY devices is difficult, and if we show a star instead of the real character typed, the user may be unsure that he's entered the text correctly (even if, as some devices do, the character is displayed for a second before it's changed to a star). If you still want to use the password input, I recommend forcing the text input to be numeric. Jakob Nielsen (*http://useit.com*), guru of web usability, agrees. In a 2009 Alertbox column, Nielsen wrote: "Usability suffers when users type in passwords and the only feedback they get is a row of bullets. Typically, masking passwords doesn't even increase security, but it does cost you business due to login failures." Facebook mobile has implemented a feature that when you misspell the password once, the next try will have a visible password input with a legend confirming that the password is still secure while visible. Another solution is to use a normal text field for the password and then add a checkbox with the label: "Hide my password" that will change the input to `password` when checked.

New HTML5 Attributes

It's safe to use any HTML5 attribute on our text fields, as they will work on compatible devices and will do nothing on older browsers. Inside the list of new form control attributes we can mention `required`, `pattern`, `placeholder`, and `min` and `max` (useful only for `<input type="number">`).

Therefore if a field is mandatory, we can mark it with the Boolean `required` attribute. And we can also define a `placeholder`, text that will be displayed grayed out—as a hint—while there is no value on the input control:

```
<div data-role="fieldcontainer">
<label for="name">Your Name:</label>
<input type="text" id="name" required placeholder="Enter your name">
</div>

<div data-role="fieldcontainer">
<label for="age">Your Age:</label>
<input type="number" id="age" required placeholder="Enter your age" min="10"
max="110">
</div>
```

Using CSS3's new pseudoclasses, we can create different styles for valid, invalid, required, and optional text fields without any JavaScript validation code.

Date Fields

Entering dates in HTML was always a problem and we used to rely on JavaScript libraries rendering visual calendars using HTML. HTML5 now has added support for date fields through the `input` element using the following types:

- `date` for a date selector (day, month, year)
- `datetime` for a complete date selector (day, month, year, hour, minutes) using standard syntax including GMT time zone
- `time` for a time selector (hour, minutes)
- `datetime-local` for a complete date selector without time zone information
- `month` for a month selector (typically rendered as a drop-down list)
- `week` for a week of the year selector (typically rendered as a drop-down list)

Date input types are new and they are not implemented on every browser, whether mobile or desktop. As of this writing, most date input types work properly on Safari for iOS since version 5.0, BlackBerry Browser for PlayBook and for Smartphones since 5.0, Opera Mobile, and Firefox for Android. You can check updated information about this compatibility at *http://mobilehtml5.org*.

 Even if we are not providing an explicit `data-role`, remember that input controls are rendered as jQuery Mobile's controls. Therefore, global attributes such as `data-theme` for color swatch definition will still work.

Remember that if the browser does not support the `input` element, it will automatically fall back to a text input:

```
<div data-role="fieldcontainer">
<label for="birth">Your Birthdate:</label>
<input type="date" id="birth" name="birth">

<label for="favmonth">Your favorite month:</label>
<input type="month" id="favmonth" name="favmonth">
</div>
```

Date input types support `min` and `max` attributes. In Figure 5-5 we can see how date fields render on some smartphones and tablets.

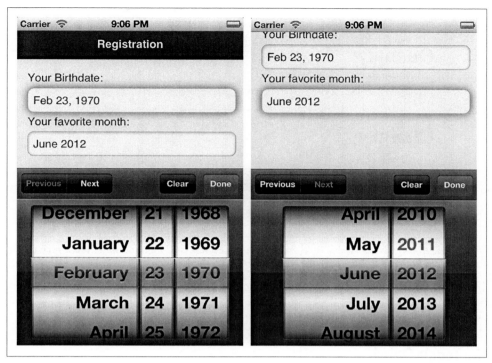

Figure 5-5. From iOS version 5 on, date elements are supported, so we will get a nice date picker when using this HTML5 input type

Slider

A slider is ideal for numeric values inside a range. When used, it provides a numeric text field and a horizontal slider at the right, as seen in Figure 5-6. To use a slider, we must define an HTML5 `<input type="range">` control. It accepts min, `max`, and `step` values:

```
<div data-role="fieldcontainer">
<label for="qty">Quantity:</label>
<input type="range" id="qty" name="qty" min="1" max="100" value="5">
</div>
```

The slider supports a color swatch definition via `data-theme` that affects the numeric input type, and we can also define a `data-track-theme` that affects only the track, as seen in Figure 5-6:

```
<div data-role="fieldcontainer">
<label for="qty">Quantity:</label>
<input type="range" id="qty" name="qty" min="1" max="100" value="5" data-theme="e"
data-track-theme="b">
</div>
```

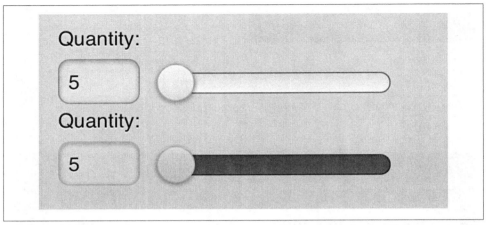

Figure 5-6. A range input type is rendered by jQuery Mobile as a numeric small input type and a synchronized horizontal slider over the standard HTML5 rendering

The slider control supports keyboard events for compatible devices. Therefore, when the control is focused, the user can use the arrow keys, wheel, or joystick to increase or decrease the control's value.

Flip Toggle Switch

A flip toggle switch is a selector for Boolean values (true or false, on or off), similar to a checkbox in functionality but with a radically different user interface. It is rendered as a visual switch that can be turned on or off by the user (tapping or dragging the switch).

This is the first form control that needs an explicit `data-role: slider`. It needs a `select` element with only two `options` as children: first the off/false value and then the on/true value:

```
<label for="updated">Receive updates</label>
<select id="updated" name="updated" data-role="slider">
<option value="no">No</option>
<option value="yes">Yes</option>
</select>
```

Without a field container, the flip toggle switch is rendered using the full page width. With a field container wrapping the content, it takes a more common visual approach, as seen in Figure 5-7.

 The HTML5 `<input type="color">` color picker control doesn't work on most mobile browsers and it will render just as any other text input control.

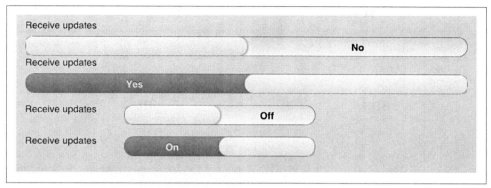

Figure 5-7. The flip toggle switch has a different width when used with a field container

Select Menus

Menus through `select` elements are a typical form control to select one or multiple options from a pop-up list. Every mobile browser supports selects (single and multiple selection). jQuery Mobile changes the `select` user interface with a button-style control that invokes the native menu when tapped, as seen in Figure 5-8.

By default, `select` menus take up the entire width unless a field container is used to wrap them:

```
<label for="training">Training</label>
<select id="training" name="training">
<option value="1">HTML5</option>
<option value="2">jQuery Mobile</option>
<option value="3">iOS</option>
<option value="4">Android</option>
<option value="5">BlackBerry</option>
<option value="6">Qt for Meego</option>
</select>
```

Using the `multiple` Boolean attribute, jQuery mobile and the native control will provide a different user interface for multiple selection, as seen in Figure 5-9:

```
<label for="lang">Languages you like</label>
<select id="lang" name="lang" multiple>
<option value="1">C/C++</option>
<option value="2">Objective-C</option>
<option value="3">Java</option>
<option value="4">C#</option>
<option value="5">Visual Basic</option>
<option value="6">ActionScript</option>
<option value="7">Delphi</option>
<option value="8">Phyton</option>
<option value="9">JavaScript</option>
<option value="10">Ruby</option>
<option value="11">PHP</option>
</select>
```

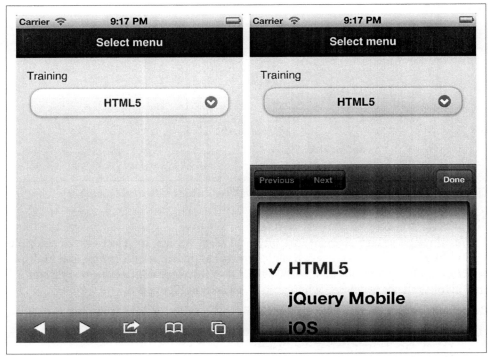

Figure 5-8. A select menu is automatically converted to a button-like style control with an icon inviting the user to open the selection menu

As any other form element, we can change the default color swatch using `data-theme`, and the `optgroup` element is also compatible for grouping option elements.

 If we change form control values from JavaScript, such as the `value` attribute of select menus, or `checked` attribute on radio buttons and checkboxes, the jQuery Mobile UI will not update unless we refresh the widgets using the jQuery Mobile API that we will cover in the next chapter.

Grouping select menus

Select menus can be grouped using the `controlgroup` element, vertically or horizontally. The latest is useful for short length selects, for example: a group of month/day/year selects. To group select menus, we need to embed them in a `div` with `data-role="controlgroup"`, as in the following examples, shown in Figure 5-10:

```
<div data-role="controlgroup">
<legend>Color and Size</legend>
<select id="color" name="color">
<option value="1">Blue</option>
```

Figure 5-9. When using a multiple selection menu, the user interface shows us the selected elements separated by a comma and a count bubble showing how many elements were selected

```
<option value="2">White</option>
<option value="3">Red</option>
<option value="4">Black</option>
<option value="5">Pink</option>
</select>
<select id="size" name="size">
<option value="1">X-Small</option>
<option value="2">Small</option>
<option value="3">Medium</option>
<option value="4">Large</option>
<option value="5">X-Large</option>
</select>
</div>

<div data-role="controlgroup" data-type="horizontal">
<legend>Week day and time</legend>
<select id="weekday" name="weekday" multiple>
<option value="1">Mon</option>
<option value="2">Tue</option>
<option value="3">Wed</option>
<option value="4">Thu</option>
<option value="5">Fri</option>
</select>
<select id="time" name="time">
<option value="1">Morning</option>
<option value="2">Midday</option>
<option value="3">Afternoon</option>
</select>
```

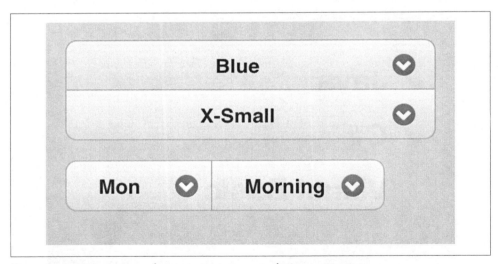

Figure 5-10. We can group select menus using a controlgroup wrapper

When using the controlgroup element, individual labels are hidden from the UI as when
used alone. To define a label for the whole group, we can use the legend element, as in
the following sample shown in Figure 5-11:

Figure 5-11. For not-so-long select menus, we can use a horizontal controlgroup element

```
<div data-role="controlgroup" data-type="horizontal">
<legend>Delivery options</legend>

<label for="weekday">Week day</label>
<select id="weekday" name="weekday" multiple>
<option value="1">Mon</option>
<option value="2">Tue</option>
<option value="3">Wed</option>
<option value="4">Thu</option>
<option value="5">Fri</option>
</select>
<label for="time">Time</label>
<select id="time" name="time">
<option value="1">Morning</option>
<option value="2">Midday</option>
<option value="3">Afternoon</option>
</select>
</div>
```

Non-native select menus

As we've already seen in Figure 5-10, every `select` element renders by default as a jQuery Mobile rich control, but when opened it relies on the native `select` element of the mobile browser. If we want to override the native behavior, jQuery Mobile provides an alternative user interface for select menus.

To activate this feature, we need to use `data-native-menu="false"` on the `select` element. As we see in Figure 5-12, it seems the same when closed, but when it's opened, the different UI appears on screen:

```
<label for="training">Training</label>
<select id="training" name="training" data-native-menu="false">
<option value="1">HTML5</option>
<option value="2">jQuery Mobile</option>
<option value="3">iOS</option>
<option value="4">Android</option>
<option value="5">BlackBerry</option>
<option value="6">Qt for Meego</option>
</select>
```

The appearance of the control is also different when we have a list with a length longer than the screen, using a dialog-like appearance, as we can see in Figure 5-13.

 When using non-native menus, `optgroup` elements will be rendered as list dividers rows as in a list view.

The non-native menus use an overlay over the current form when it's open. We have the `data-overlay-theme` to define the color swatch for this overlay. If we have an `option` element with an explicit empty value, `value=""`, or with the data-

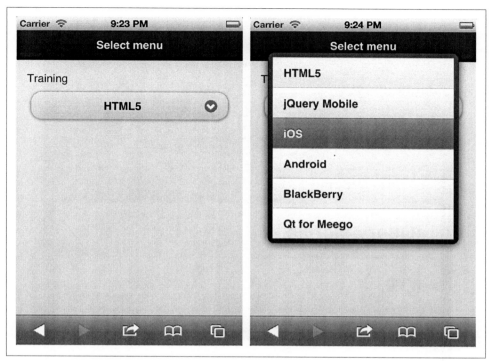

Figure 5-12. When using a non-native select menu, the original menu is replaced by an interactive list view on a dialog-like mode

`placeholder="true"` attribute, it will be used as the overlay's title and not a selectable option, as in the following sample (Figure 5-14):

```
<label for="training">Training</label>
<select id="training" name="training" data-native-menu="false" data-overlay-theme="e">
<option value="0" data-placeholder="true">Select your training</option>
<option value="1">HTML5</option>
<option value="2">jQuery Mobile</option>
<option value="3">iOS</option>
<option value="4">Android</option>
<option value="5">BlackBerry</option>
<option value="6">Qt for Meego</option>
</select>
```

As we can see in Figure 5-15, non-native menus also work nicely with multiple selection menus, with the `multiple` Boolean attribute defined. When `multiple` is defined, the overlay dialog will have a close button, instead of an automatic close after a selection.

jQuery Mobile also detects the `disabled` attribute for `option` elements properly.

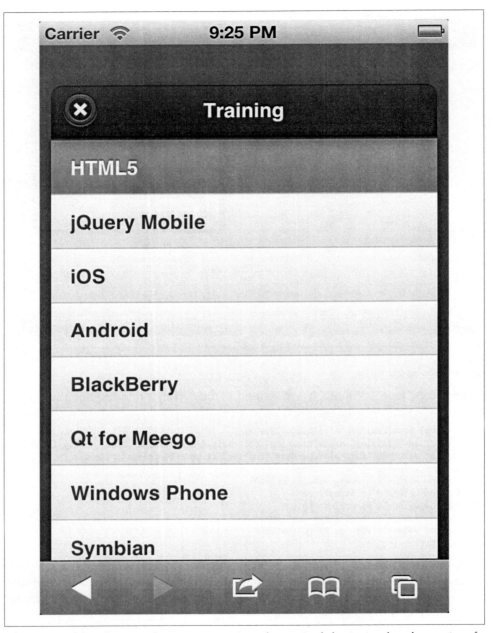

Figure 5-13. If the select menu has too many options, the opening behavior involves the creation of a dialog page

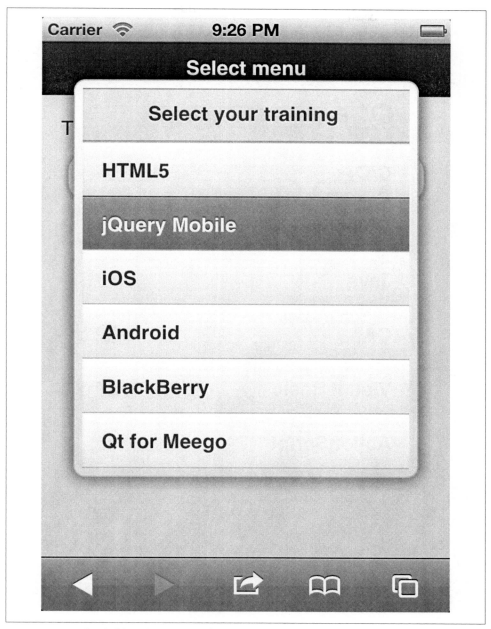

Figure 5-14. A placeholder allows us to define a title for the selection dialog in a non-native select list

Figure 5-15. Multiple non-native menus have a user interface with a multiple selection list view

For non-native menus to work, we have one restriction on `option` elements. They need to include explicitly the `value` attribute with an option. If you define an empty `value`, then it will be used as the title of the pop-over window.

Radio Buttons

We all know what a radio button is. The great thing about radio buttons on jQuery Mobile is how they are rendered without any work from us. First, let's check the requirements for radio buttons to work properly on jQuery Mobile:

- Every option must be a `<input type="radio">`.
- Every option of the same group must have the same `name` value.
- Every option must have a unique `id` and a unique `label` element applied to it.

One big difference between using select menus and radio buttons is that with `select`, the label applies to the whole element, while on radio buttons the label applies to each element. In Figure 5-16 we can see that the label is part of the button text and it's not a label outside the control, as in an input text control.

If we want to provide a label to a whole group of options, we can use the `legend` HTML element.

Let's see a sample:

```
<legend>Menu type</legend>

<label for="menuNative1">Native menu, single selection</label>
<input type="radio" id="menuNative1" name="menuType" value="1">

<label for="menuNative2">Native menu, multiple selection</label>
<input type="radio" id="menuNative2" name="menuType" value="2">

<label for="menuNonNative1">Non-native menu, single selection</label>
<input type="radio" id="menuNonNative1" name="menuType" value="3">

<label for="menuNonNative2">Non-native menu, multiple selection</label>
<input type="radio" id="menuNonNative2" name="menuType" value="4">
```

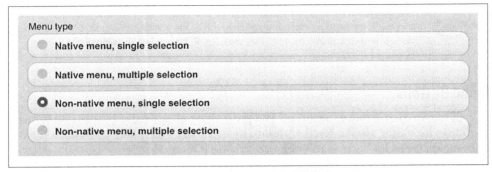

Figure 5-16. Radio buttons are rendered with their labels inside a button

If we embed every radio element inside a `controlgroup` wrapper, then we'll have a nicer UI, as seen in Figure 5-17:

```
<div data-role="controlgroup">
<-- label and radio elements go here -->
</div>
```

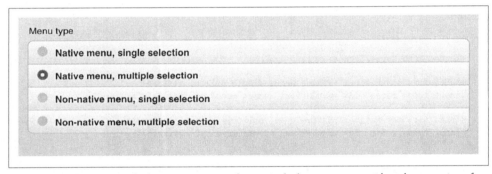

Figure 5-17. Grouping radio buttons in a controlgroup is the best way to provide a clear user interface

If we change the `controlgroup` element's type to `horizontal`, then we have a very different appearance. The elements will not have the typical radio selector, and the control will become a pushed button control, as seen in Figure 5-18:

```
<legend>Delivery method</legend>

<div data-role="controlgroup" data-type="horizontal">

<label for="deliveryUPS">UPS</label>
<input type="radio" id="deliveryUPS" name="delivery" value="ups">

<label for="deliveryDHL">DHL</label>
<input type="radio" id="deliveryDHL" name="delivery" value="dhl">
```

```
<label for="deliveryFedex">FedEx</label>
<input type="radio" id="deliveryFedex" name="delivery" value="fedex">

</div>
```

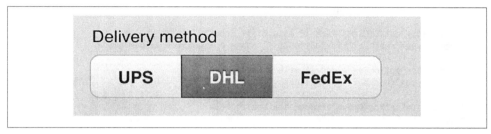

Figure 5-18. Using a horizontal controlgroup wrapper, radio buttons are converted to pushed buttons using a different color swatch for the selected value

 Even if jQuery Mobile presents the radio button user interface completely differently, the form is still working in the same way. That means that the value property will match the selected value element.

Checkboxes

Checkboxes work similarly to radio buttons (Figure 5-19), but with multiple selection. We can use a single checkbox as in the following sample:

```
<label for="accept">I accept terms and conditions</label>
<input type="checkbox" id="accept" name="accept" value="yes">
```

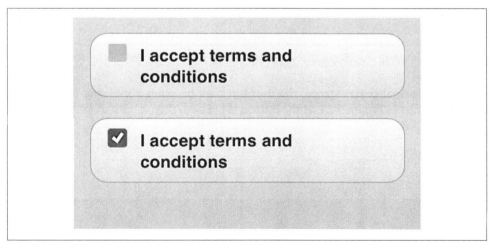

Figure 5-19. A checkbox takes its label and renders a nice button with a checkbox button while selected

We can also wrap checkboxes inside a `controlgroup` and we will have a grouped buttons user interface with multiple selection (Figure 5-20):

```
<legend>Delivery options</legend>

<div data-role="controlgroup">

<label for="optionGift">Pack it as a Gift</label>
<input type="checkbox" id="optionGift" name="optionGift" value="yes">

<label for="optionBag">Send it with a bag</label>
<input type="checkbox" id="optionBag" name="optionBag" value="yes">

<label for="optionRemove">Remove the box</label>
<input type="checkbox" id="optionRemove" name="optionRemove" value="yes">

</div>
```

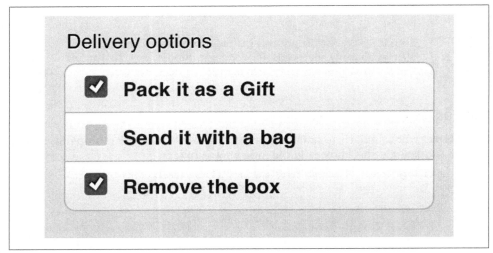

Figure 5-20. Grouping checkboxes with a legend element creates a nice multiple selection list.

Using a horizontal `controlgroup`, the user interface becomes a multiple push-button control, as seen in Figure 5-21. If the button is pressed, then it's a checked element.

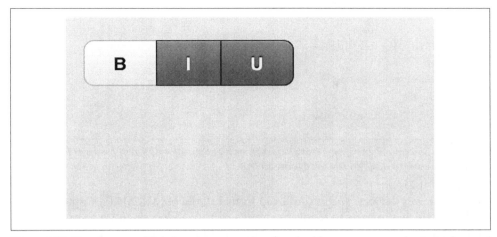

Figure 5-21. If we have small labels and not more than five checkboxes, we can use horizontal control group wrappers to have a push-button multiple selection control

```
<div data-role="controlgroup" data-type="horizontal">

<label for="bold">B</label>
<input type="checkbox" id="bold" name="bold" value="yes">

<label for="italic">I</label>
<input type="checkbox" id="italic" name="italic" value="yes">

<label for="underline">U</label>
<input type="checkbox" id="underline" name="underline" value="yes">

</div>
```

File Uploads

File uploads are a real problem in the mobile space, and it's because lack of compatibility on some smartphones and tablet platforms, such as iOS (iPhone and iPad), Android before 2.2, and webOS (Figure 5-22). These platforms don't support `<input type="file">` for different reasons, including the lack of a user-public filesystem. jQuery Mobile doesn't provide any specific appearance for file uploads, and we should be very careful implementing them on mobile browsers.

Figure 5-22. Some mobile browsers and platforms, such as Safari for iOS, don't support file uploads, and we will receive a disabled standard form control

On some newer devices, such as Android from 3.0, the HTML Media Capture API is available, which allows us to request a camera picture, video, or audio recording from a file upload input type. You can check *http://mobilehtml5.org* for compatibility with this HTML5 API.

## CHAPTER 6

The Framework and JavaScript

jQuery Mobile provides a JavaScript API to communicate with the framework and to manage content using JavaScript. The first thing to know is that the framework is an HTML5 framework and the best way to create content is by using nonintrusive HTML5.

Creating pages and content using JavaScript instead of markup will lead to incompatibilities with some B-grade browsers and with older non-jQuery Mobile compatible platforms. If you are targeting modern tablets and smartphones and you are prepared to test your code on different real devices, then it's safe to create content using JavaScript and AJAX instead of markup directly.

The JavaScript API not only allows us to create dynamic content compatible with the framework, but it also enables new events for us to handle and global configurations that we can define.

This chapter will require a basic knowledge of JavaScript and the jQuery core framework.

Document Events

It's common on a web page to use the load event to configure some defaults and initialization code. If you are using the jQuery core framework, you may also be fond of the ready event exposed to the document element.

When we are working with a jQuery Mobile document, we have a new event that we need to handle and to understand: mobileinit. This new event will be fired when the jQuery Mobile framework is loaded and ready for our initialization code. This event should be handled on the document element using jQuery's bind method:

```
$(document).bind('mobileinit', function() {
    // Initialization code here
});
```

Mobile initialization is fired after the jQuery Mobile framework is loaded into memory and just before rendering the UI elements. That is why we can use this event handler to change some of the UI global preferences.

The order of a jQuery Mobile document's event execution usually is:

- `mobileinit`
- `ready`
- `load`

 If you want to execute some code after a page is loaded or shown, you should not use `load`, `ready`, or `mobileinit`. Every jQuery Mobile page element has a series of events that we can bind to.

The first thing to discuss about the `mobileinit` event is where should it be placed. We should bind this event in a special place inside the `header` element. It should be between the jQuery core include and the jQuery Mobile include. That is because we need the `$` jQuery object to be ready and we need to bind it before the jQuery Mobile framework is executed.

That is why the typical template for a jQuery Mobile document with a script configuration code is:

```
<!DOCTYPE html>
<html>
  <head>
        <meta charset="utf-8" />
        <title>My first jQuery Mobile code</title>
        <link rel="stylesheet" href="http://code.jquery.com/mobile/1.0/jquery.mobile-
1.0.min.css" />
        <script src="http://code.jquery.com/jquery-1.6.4.min.js"></script>

        <!-- CUSTOM INITIALIZATION CODE -->
        <script src="customcode.js"></script>

        <script src="http://code.jquery.com/mobile/1.0/jquery.mobile-
1.0.min.js"></script>
      <meta name="viewport" content="width=device-width, initial-scale=1">
  </head>
</html>
```

Keep in mind that adding too many `script` tags on a mobile page is a bad practice because of performance issues. In some situations it's better to have all the custom initialization code as an inline script code inside the HTML document instead of having it in an external file.

If you are working with external documents, be aware that the script tags on the external documents loaded via AJAX will not be executed unless the user is accessing your website not from the home page, so everything should be declared in one JavaScript external file and linked from every document.

For example, we can bind `mobileinit` event as in the following sample:

```
<script src="http://code.jquery.com/jquery-1.6.4.min.js"></script>

<script>
$(document).bind("mobileinit", function() {
        // Our initialization code here
});
<script>

<script src="http://code.jquery.com/mobile/1.0/jquery.mobile-
1.0.min.js"></script>
```

Configuration

jQuery Mobile attaches a new `mobile` object to the jQuery main object, `$`, also available as `jQuery`. Therefore, most of the work with the API will be done using `$.mobile` or `jQuery.mobile`. We will find global attributes and useful methods to use and call while creating our jQuery Mobile experience. This object will only be available after a `mobileinit` event is fired.

The framework uses the widget architecture of the jQuery UI framework for desktop. A widget is a control that is managed by the framework. In jQuery Mobile 1.0, the widgets available are usually mapped from a `data-role` attribute, but we have the form controls without a role, too. Therefore, `page`, `button`, and `listview` are widgets inside the framework.

Every widget has an object constructor and default configuration that we can change inside the `mobileinit` that affects every widget instance on the page.

The following is the list of widgets available in jQuery Mobile 1.0:

- `page`
- `dialog`
- `collapsible`
- `fieldcontain`
- `navbar`
- `listview`
- `checkboxradio`
- `button`

- slider
- textinput
- selectmenu
- controlgroup

Some jQuery Mobile rich controls are grouped in one widget; for example, all the text input types—even `textarea`—use the same widget: `textinput`. Checkboxes and radio buttons are also grouped in the `checkboxradio` widget.

Every widget has its own object constructor that represents how every object on the page will work. We can access this prototype using `$.mobile.<widget_name>.proto type`. Usually, every widget constructor has an `option` object where we can define widget default attributes, for example, `$.mobile.page.prototype.options` to define default attributes that will be applied to every page instance (`data-role="page"`).

 Remember to set up global defaults or widget defaults on the `mobileinit` event handler. If we change defaults after or before, the new attributes may not be applied to our document.

Global Configuration

A lot of values that we can define using a `data-*` attribute explicitly on every element, can be defined globally to be applied to every control, unless a new value is defined in the markup.

Most of the global configuration values can be changed via `$.mobile` object, in the `mobileinit` event handler.

User interface

By default, jQuery Mobile assigns classes to specific elements on the page and other classes while the elements are active. These classes are used by the theme stylesheet to provide different appearances. We can change the class name used by the current active page (in a multipage document) or the class name used by an active button by using the string-based properties `activePageClass` and `activeBtnClass`. By default, the values are `ui-page-active` and `ui-btn-active`. The active button state is used on many other widgets, such as navigation bars, radio buttons, and checkboxes using buttons internally.

There are two global attributes (which we will not change in most situations) that allow us to change scrolling behavior. By default, when a jQuery Mobile document is loaded, it is scrolled down from the top just enough to hide the address bar. We can change this by setting the `defaultHomeScroll` value. When we open a page and then go back again to it, the framework scrolls the viewport to the same position where the original page was in the first tap (remembering the position). However, if the first page was very near to the top (but not at the pixel 0), the framework will stay at the top and not scroll.

The default minimum value to scroll while going back is defined as 250 pixels high; we can change it using the `minScrollBack` attribute.

Finally, two global attributes that we will change more frequently are the default transitions applied to page loading and dialog loading. By default, they are assigned to `slide` and `pop` and we can change them using `defaultPageTransition` and `defaultDialogTransition` attributes.

The following example will change some user interface default values:

```
$(document).bind("mobileinit", function() {
        // We change default values
        $.mobile.defaultPageTransition = "fade";
        $.mobile.minScrollBack = 150;
        $.mobile.activeBtnClass = "active-button";
});
```

Core and AJAX functionalities

Some of the core functionalities of the framework can be manipulated through some global attributes. We can define a namespace via the `ns` global attribute if we are using another framework that can conflict with jQuery Mobile. By default the namespace is not defined. If we define a namespace, for example:

```
$(document).bind("mobileinit", function() {
        // We change default values
        $.mobile.ns = "firt";
});
```

Then, all the `data-*` attributes become `data-<namespace>-*`—for example `data-firt-*` in our case—including every jQuery Mobile custom attribute such as `data-role` (converted to `data-<namespace>-role`). With our new namespace, the typical page template should be:

```
<div data-firt-role="page">
    <div data-firt-role="header" data-firt-theme="a">

    </div>
    <div data-firt-role="content">

    </div>
</div>
```

 If you define a namespace, you should also manually change the CSS file (both structural and theme files) to understand your new namespace. For example, you should replace [data-role=page] conditional selectors to match your new namespace, such as [data-namespace-role=page].

One of the core functionalities of jQuery Mobile is the AJAX framework used to load external pages. We can disable all the AJAX functionality using the Boolean attribute ajaxEnabled. If we disable it with `$.mobile.ajaxEnabled=false`, then every external page will be loaded as a full HTTP request on the browser.

By default, `XMLHttpRequest`—the object behind AJAX—doesn't allow cross-domain requests. That means that if our page is on *domain1.com*, we can't load a page using AJAX from *domain2.com*. The framework automatically uses a full HTTP request in this situation. There are some special situations where we can still use cross-domain requests and we can force the framework to support that through the `allowCrossDomainPages` attributes.

 Some new mobile browsers support Cross Origin Resource Sharing (CORS), a W3C working draft available at *http://w3.org/TR/cors*. This standard allows a browser to support a cross-domain request if the second server response includes some special HTTP headers. You can check *http://mobilehtml5.org* to verify compatibility of CORS inside mobile browsers.

If you are creating an offline application or a hybrid solution—such as a PhoneGap or RhoMobile application—you are basically loading pages through the `file://` protocol (local files). These frameworks allows you to perform AJAX requests to any domain on the Internet, so if you are creating this kind of application and want to load external pages from the Web, you should allow it using `$.mobile.allowCrossDomainPages=true`.

Some widgets, such as nested list views, generate new pages dynamically. The framework needs a name for every new page (for hash, URL, and other purposes). By default, jQuery Mobile uses `ui-page` as the parameter name, unless we change it using `subPa geUrlKey` from the `$.mobile` object. When talking about dialogs, we have the property `dialogHashKey` that is by default linked to `ui-state=dialog`. Usually, we won't change these properties.

If you want the framework to not change every link behavior to support different actions from jQuery Mobile, you can disable it by using `$.mobile.linkBindingEnabled=false`. By default, jQuery Mobile initializes the first page in the document after the DOM is ready. We can disable this behavior by using `$.mobile.autoInitializePage=false`.

We can also disable the automatic hash reading that allows automatic forward and back actions when the user presses the browser or device's back and forward buttons using `$.mobile.hashListeningEnabled=false`.

Localizable strings

The framework has some hard-coded string values inside the framework that we can change or localize to other languages. Some of them are not visible on a typical jQuery Mobile document and that is because they are used for semantic information or for accessibility (so screen readers can say what are they).

The possible strings to change include the loading message when an external page is loading via AJAX, the page load error message when the external page can't be loaded, and some other widget-based messages.

The following is the list of messages with the default value:

```
// Global strings
$.mobile.loadingMessage = "loading";
$.mobile.pageLoadErrorMessage = "Error Loading Page";

// Widget strings
$.mobile.page.prototype.options.backBtnText = "Back";
$.mobile.dialog.prototype.options.closeBtnText = "Close"
$.mobile.collapsible.prototype.options.expandCueText =
  " click to expand contents";
$.mobile.collapsible.prototype.options. collapseCueText = " click to collapse contents";
$.mobile.listview.prototype.options.filterPlaceholder = "Filter items...";
$.mobile.selectmenu.prototype.options.closeText = "Close";
```

Therefore, to create a Spanish version of the jQuery Mobile's texts, we should use the following code:

```
$(document).bind('mobileinit', function() {
  // Global strings
  $.mobile.loadingMessage = "cargando";
  $.mobile.pageLoadErrorMessage = "Error Cargando Página";

  // Widget strings
  $.mobile.page.prototype.options.backBtnText = "Atrás";
  $.mobile.dialog.prototype.options.closeBtnText = "Cerrar"
  $.mobile.collapsible.prototype.options.expandCueText =
    " click para expandir contenido";
  $.mobile.collapsible.prototype.options. collapseCueText =
    " click para cerrar contenido";
  $.mobile.listview.prototype.options.filterPlaceholder = "Filtrar ítems...";
  $.mobile.selectmenu.prototype.options.closeText = "Cerrar";

});
```

Touch overflow

As we have discussed in previous chapters, enabling fixed toolbars (with `data-posi tion="fixed"`) doesn't provide a real fixed toolbar in jQuery Mobile 1.0. It just emulates a fixed toolbar while not scrolling the page. See Figure 6-1.

As of iOS 5.0, Safari supports `position: fixed` elements and one-finger scrolling over block areas with `overflow: scroll` and a new prefix-based extension, called `overflow-scrolling: touch`. By default, this behavior is disabled, but if we want to provide real fixed toolbars on iOS 5 (and possibly other platforms in the future), we just need to enable `touchOverflowEnabled`. It will fall back to a normal jQuery Mobile fixed toolbar on noncompatible platforms:

```
$(document).bind('mobileinit', function() {
    $.mobile.touchOverflowEnabled=true;
});
```

 Scrolling inside block elements with `overflow: scroll` is also supported on Android 3.0 and BlackBerry Browser for PlayBook. jQuery Mobile will add automatic support for these browsers after 1.1.

If we enable this property, we can also enable zooming using `touchOverflow ZoomEnabled`. Be careful with this option because it can lead to some usability problems. These two properties should become obsolete in later versions because they will be replaced by a default fixed toolbar behavior.

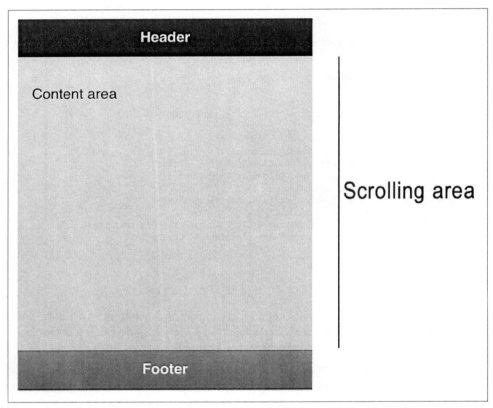

Figure 6-1. When we use touch overflow fixed headers, the page is designed in a different way: the content area has its own scrolling area

Page Configuration

For every page, `data-role="page"` is created using default options that can be overridden by `data-*` attributes. If we want to change defaults, we can change the prototype's options of every page instance.

For example, if we want to provide a visible back button on every page that has a previous history page, we can define the `addBackBtn` property as `true`. We can change the back button's text and theme through `backBtnText` and `backBtnTheme`.

And we can also change the default theme by defining `headerTheme`, `footerTheme`, and `contentTheme`.

For example:

```
$(document).bind('mobileinit', function() {
  $.mobile.page.prototype.options.addBackBtn  = true;
  $.mobile.page.prototype.options.backBtnTheme = "e";
  $.mobile.page.prototype.options.headerTheme  = "b";
  $.mobile.page.prototype.options.footerTheme  = "d";
});
```

 If you are creating a full-screen webapp, a hybrid, or a PhoneGap app, you should definitely provide an explicit back button in the header, so you must handle `mobileinit` event and define `$.mobile.page.proto type.options.addBackBtn=true`.

Page loading

Every time a page is externally loaded using AJAX, some default attributes are used. These attributes can be found in `$.mobile.loadPage.defaults` object, and Table 6-1 shows its possible values.

Table 6-1. $.mobile.loadPage.defaults properties

Property	Accepting	Default value	Description
type	"get"/"post"	"get"	Defines the AJAX request type
data	object/string		If type is "post", this is where we can set the post object to send
reloadPage	true/false	false	Defines whether the new page should be reloaded even if it's cached on the DOM
role	string	<defined by data-role>	Defines the role to apply to the target page
showLoadMsg	true/false	true	Defines whether the loading message should be visible if

Property	Accepting	Default value	Description
			the request is taking longer than the timeout defined
loadMsgDelay	milliseconds	50	Milliseconds to wait before showing the loading message
theme	a to z	c	Default color swatch to apply to every page
domCache	true/false	false	Defines whether pages should be cached on the DOM

 If we want to change a page loading attribute just for one page load and not for all, we can use the `$.mobile.changePage` utility.

Widgets Configuration

Every widget on jQuery Mobile has its own default configuration attributes. Remember we can change its defaults by changing the `options` object of the widget's prototype, `$.mobile.<widget_name>.prototype.options`. For example:

```
$(document).bind('mobileinit', function() {
    // Enables filtering on all the listviews
    $.mobile.listview.prototype.filter = true;

    // Enables non-native menus for all selects
    $.mobile.selectmenu.prototype.nativeMenu=false;
});
```

 Most widgets support the `theme` default attribute. Therefore, if we want all select menus to have the e theme by default, we can use `$.mobile.selectmenu.prototype.theme="e"`.

Table 6-2 shows the most commonly used attributes for each widget that we can change.

Table 6-2. Default properties available to define for every widget.

Widget	Property	Values (default)	Description
<every widget>	theme	a to z	Color swatch to be applied to every widget's instance
listview	filter	true/(false)	Enables filtering on every list view

Widget	Property	Values (default)	Description
listview	filterPlaceHolder	string	Placeholder text of the filter's text box
listview	filterTheme	a to z	Color Swatch for the filter text box
navbar	iconpos	(top)/bottom/left/right	Icon position for navigation bar's items
slider	trackTheme	a to z	Color swatch for the track of the slider
selectmenu	icon	icon value (arrow_d)	Icon for the select's opening button
selectmenu	iconpos	top/bottom/left/(right)	Icon position
selectmenu	corners	(true)/false	Rounded corners for the opening button
selectmenu	shadow	(true)/false	Shadow for the opening button
selectmenu	iconshadow	(true)/false	Shadow for the opening button's icon
selectmenu	menuPageTheme	a to z (b)	Color swatch for the non-native menu
selectmenu	overlayTheme	a to z (a)	Color swatch for the non-native overlay
selectmenu	closeText	string	String for the close button for non-native menus
selectmenu	nativeMenu	(true)/false	Defines whether the select menus will be native or not
dialog	closeBtnText	string	String for the close button
dialog	overlayTheme	a to z (a)	Color swatch for the dialog overlay
collapsible	expandCueText	string	Text for the opening button
collapsible	collapseCueText	string	Text for the closing button
collapsible	collapsed	(true)/false	Defines whether the collapsible should be opened or closed by default
collapsible	heading	comma-separated values	List of tags that will be used as collapsible's header
collapsible	contentTheme	a to z	Color swatch for the content
collapsible	iconTheme	a to z	Color swatch for the header's icon

Widget	Property	Values (default)	Description
button	icon	icon value	By default icon for every button
button	iconpos	icon position	Icon position for every button
button	inline	true/(false)	Defines whether every button should be inline or not
button	corners	(true)/false	Rounded corners for every button
button	shadow	(true)/false	Shadow for every button
button	iconshadow	(true)/false	Shadow for the button's icon

Utilities

jQuery Mobile provides lot of utilities for managing our application from JavaScript. Utilities are provided by methods and read-only attributes that will allow us to create better experiences from JavaScript.

Data-* Utilities

When using jQuery Mobile, it's common to manipulate data-* custom attributes extensively. For example, if we are trying to get a collection of buttons on the page, we can use jQuery:

```
var buttons = $("a[data-role=button]");
```

jQuery Mobile adds a new jQuery Mobile filter called jqmData that also applies a namespace if we are using one. It's safer and easy to change the previous code with:

```
var buttons = $("a:jqmData(role='button')");
```

jqmData and jqmRemoveData should also be used instead of the typical jQuery functions data and removeData on a jQuery collection object, for example:

```
$("a").jqmRemoveData("transition");
$("#button1").jqmData("theme", "a");
```

Page Utilities

If we need to access the current page, jQuery Mobile provides the $.mobile.active Page attribute that is automatically linked to the current visible data-role="page" element. This property is linked to the jQuery DOM object (usually a div element):

```
var currentPageId = $.mobile.activePage.id;
```

We can access the current page container (usually the body element) with the $.mobile.pageContainer attribute.

The most useful utility on the framework is the `$.mobile.changePage` method. It allows us to transition to another page as if the user clicked a link. We can use this method to show both internal and external pages using JavaScript.

 Some utilities are only available after a `mobileinit` event is fired. So we can't use them inside this event handler.

The first mandatory parameter can be a string value (meaning a URL for an external page) or a jQuery object with an internal page.

To load an external page *external.html* we can just use:

```
$.mobile.changePage("external.html");
```

To transition to an internal page already in the same document, we can use:

```
$.mobile.changePage($("#pageId"));
```

 We cannot open internal pages just by loading them as a string `"#pageId"`, we have to send the DOM object using jQuery, `$("#pageId")`.

Page transition options

The second optional argument of `changePage` is an object, usually defined with JSON syntax, with optional attributes for the transition and/or AJAX loading.

All the possible options are defined in Table 6-3.

Table 6-3. Optional properties available for a changePage operation

Property	Values	Default value	Description
transition	transition name	slide	Transition to be applied
reverse	true/false	false	Defines if the transition should be done in reverse (usually for back actions)
type	"get"/"post"	"get"	HTTP method to use to load the external page
data	object or string		Data to be sent when POST is defined
allowSamePageTransition	true/false	false	Allow transition to the same page as the active one (transition to itself)
changeHash	true/false	true	Decides if the new page should be in the history
data-url	string		The URL to be attached in the location

Property	Values	Default value	Description
pageContainer	jQuery DOM object		The container where to attach the new page
reloadPage	true/false	false	Forces a reload of the page, even if its cached on the DOM
showLoadMsg	true/false	true	Determines whether the page loading message should be visible after some milliseconds or not
role	page/dialog	defined by data-role	The role to be applied to the new page

If we want to force a reverse slide transition, we can use:

```
$.mobile.changePage($("#page2"), {
    transition: "slide",
    reverse: true
});
```

The following sample will load an external page sending data via POST:

```
<script>
function viewProduct(idProduct) {
    $.mobile.changePage("productdetail.php", {
        method: "post",
        data: {
            action: 'getProduct',
            id: idProduct
        },
        transition: "fade"
    });
}
</script>

<!-- ... -->
<a href="javascript:viewProduct(5200)" data-role="button">Product details</a>
```

 Remember that even if we are loading a page using POST, the destination must be a jQuery Mobile document, including headers and a data-role="page".

There is a $.mobile.loadPage method that is mainly used by changePage when an external page is loaded. This method will bring the target page to the DOM but will not transition to it. We should use changePage instead. We can use loadPage if we want to prefetch content, inject it on the DOM, and then use changePage in the future to transition to it with the jQuery DOM object.

Platform Utilities

The framework provides us with some platform utilities that we can use to help web development. Table 6-4 shows the most useful platform utilities.

Table 6-4. Utilities available to query about the executing platform in $.mobile object

Method/property	Description
orientationChangeEnabled	If the native orientationchange event is available.
gradeA()	Returns true if the browser is an A-grade browser in the jQuery Mobile's compatibility chart.
urlHistory	A collection of pages that were browsed inside jQuery Mobile without a page reload. Every element has pageUrl, title, and transition.
getDocumentUrl()	Returns the original document's URL (the first load).
getDocumentBase()	Returns the original document base.
keyCode	Constants defining codes for key event handling, includes: ALT, BACKSPACE, COMMAND, COMMAND_LEFT, COMMAND_RIGHT, DELETE, DOWN, UP, RIGHT, LEFT, END, ENTER, ESCAPE, HOME, INSERT, MENU, PAGE_DOWN, PAGE_UP, PERIOD, SHIFT, SPACE, TAB, WINDOWS.
getScreenHeight()	Get the current screen's height.

Path Utilities

There are some path management utilities used by the framework and exposed as public methods through $.mobile.path. The methods are shown in Table 6-5.

Table 6-5. Path utilities available in $.mobile.path object.

Method	Description
parseUrl(url)	Returns an object with every part of the URL as a property (protocol, hostname, port, pathname, directory, filename, hash, and more)
makePathAbsolute(relativePath, absolutePath)	Returns an absolute path based on a relative one
makeUrlAbsolute(relativeUrl, absoluteUrl)	Returns an absolute URL based on a relative one
isSameDomain(Url1, Url2)	Returns true if both URLs are in the same domain
isRelativeUrl(Url)	Returns true if the URL is relative
isAbsolute(Url)	Returns true if the URL is absolute

UI Utilities

The last series of utilities are for user interface. With $.mobile.getInheritedTheme(element, defaultSwatch) we can receive the color swatch that should be applied to an element based on its own color swatch definition or the inherit chain.

With $.mobile.silentScroll(y) we can scroll to any position in the page without animation and event triggering and with $.mobile.showPageLoadingMsg() and $.mobile.hidePageLoadingMsg() we can show and hide the loading message pop up by our own.

```
// This code shows the loading message and hide it after 2 seconds
$.mobile.showPageLoadingMsg();
setTimeout(function() {
    $.mobile.hidePageLoadingMsg();
}, 2000);
```

Finally, $.mobile.fixedToolbars.show() and $.mobile.fixedToolbars.hide() let us show and hide the fixed toolbars (as we have seen in previous chapters). The toolbars can be full screen or just fixed. You can't hide real fixed toolbars for iOS 5. By default, they are shown and hidden using a fade transition. We can change that by defining a true parameter so that $.mobile.fixedToolbars.show(true) will show the toolbars immediately without fade animation.

Custom Transitions

In Chapter 3 we have already mentioned all the possible transitions available in jQuery Mobile 1.0. Can we define our own transitions? Yes we can, and there are two ways:

- Using CSS3 animations
- Using JavaScript

When we define a data-transition attribute (or by applying a transition from Java-Script), jQuery Mobile first verifies if the name is one of the transitions available in the framework. If not, it looks inside a collection called $.mobile.transitionHandlers. If the transition is unknown and not defined in the collection, a default transition is used.

The default transition can be changed, and must be defined as a handler function. By default, the fallback transition is mapped to a custom transition that must be defined in CSS3 animations (see next chapter).

We can also map the default transition to $.mobile.noneTransitionHandler, which basically shows the new page and hides the previous page without any animation.

For example, we can add an explode transition type:

```
$.mobile.transitionHandlers.explode = explodeTransitionHandler;
```

We can also change the default transition and then use whatever name we want using the same handler:

```
$.mobile.defaultTransitionHandler = explodeTransitionHandler;
```

A transition handler is a JavaScript function that will receive four arguments:

- Name of the transition
- `reverse`, which when set to true, indicates when the transition should occur in reverse
- `toPage`, which is a jQuery DOM object of the destination page
- `fromPage`, which is a jQuery DOM object of the origin page

We can use whatever JavaScript code we want to make the transition. Just be sure that, at the end, you've removed the `$.mobile.activePageClass` from the origin page and you've applied it to the destination page.

 Be careful with JavaScript-based transitions. You may have compatibility and performance issues on some platforms. Do extensive testing before using them.

Dynamic Content

If we are using dynamic content, such as a database-driven website, it's possible that we don't want to create jQuery Mobile documents on the fly and we just want to use JavaScript and AJAX to change, show, and hide information in our webapp.

 When you are using JavaScript-based elements instead of semantic markup you may have problem with non-jQuery Mobile compatible browsers. If you are targeting smartphones and tablets you may not have any problem.

Creating Pages

Can we create pages on the fly? We know that a page is just a `div` element with a proper `data-role`, so our first thought is that we can make it work. Let's try and see what it happens. We are going to create a basic page that will create four pages on the fly using JavaScript:

```
<div data-role="page">
     <div data-role="header">
  <h1>Dynamic page</h1>
  </div>
     <div data-role="content">
     <a id="button1" href="javascript:addPages()" data-role="button">Add Pages</a>
     <ul id="list1">

     </ul>
  </div>
</div>
```

Then in a script we define the function to create dynamic pages and add buttons to transition to them:

```
function addPages() {
    for (var i=1; i<5; i++) {
        var page = $("<div>").jqmData("role", "page").attr("id", "page" + i);
        // header
        $("<div>").attr("data-role", "header").append($("<h1>")
            .html("Page " + i)).appendTo(page);
        // content
        $("<div>").attr("data-role", "content").append($("<p>")
            .html("Contents for page " + i))
            .appendTo(page);

        $("body").append(page);

            $("<li>").append($("<a>").attr("href", "#page"+i).html("Go to page " + i))
                .appendTo("#list1");
    }
        $("#button1").hide();
};
```

If we see this in action in Figure 6-2, we will see that if the pages are created dynamically after the page is loaded, they work but they don't have the right CSS styles for the header.

> Dynamically created pages have one disadvantage: if the user reloads the page while on one of the new pages, it will not work unless we capture mobileinit and check to see if the user (reading the hash value or a page event) is trying to load one of the dynamic pages. On a second load, this page will not exist, so we need to create it by demand.

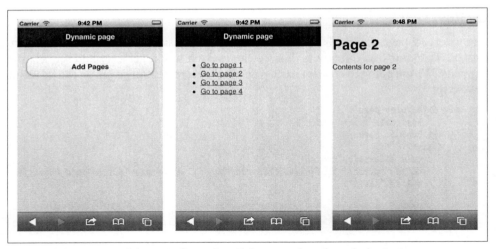

Figure 6-2. Pages created dynamically work as if they were there from the beginning

To enhance a page injected dynamically, we can call the page() method on the jQuery DOM element, for example $("#page1").page().

The preferred way to create dynamic pages is just by linking to them, for example, link to #page1 and capture pagebeforechange modifying the behavior of the framework. This event will be covered in the next pages but the following code is enough to understand it:

```
<!DOCTYPE html>
<html xmlns="http://www.w3.org/1999/xhtml">
<head>
<meta charset="UTF-8" />
<title>jQuery Mobile</title>
<script src="jquery.js"></script>
<link rel="stylesheet" type="text/css" href="jquery.mobile-1.0.css">
<script src="jquery.mobile-1.0.js"></script>
<script>
$(document).bind('pagebeforechange', function(event, data) {
        // We receive the destination page in data.toPage and we normalize it
        var url = $.mobile.path.parseUrl(data.toPage).hash;

        if (url!=undefined && url.length>5 && url.substring(0, 5)=="#page") {
                // We dynamically inject a new page
                var id = url.substring(5);

                // We will use a page template already in the DOM
                $("#pageTemplate h1").html("Page " + id);

                // We change to the real page template without using
                // its real page id in history
                $.mobile.changePage($("#pageTemplate"), {dataUrl: data.toPage});

                // We prevent normal page transition
                event.preventDefault();
        }

});

</script>
<meta name="viewport" content="width=device-width,user-scalable=no">

</head>

<body>
<div data-role="page">
        <div data-role="header">
    <h1>Dynamic pages</h1>
    </div>
        <div data-role="content">
        <a id="button1" href="#page1" data-role="button">Page 1</a>
        <a id="button1" href="#page2" data-role="button">Page 2</a>
        <a id="button1" href="#page3" data-role="button">Page 3</a>
        <a id="button1" href="#page4" data-role="button">Page 4</a>
    </div>
</div>
```

```
<div data-role="page" id="pageTemplate">
  <div data-role="header">
    <h1>Header</h1>
  </div>
  <div data-role="content">Content</div>
  <div data-role="footer">
    <h4>Footer</h4>
  </div>
</div>
</body>
</html>
```

 If we try to inject other widgets using JavaScript while the page is being rendered, they may not be rendered properly until we fire the create event.

Creating Widgets

If we look at Figure 6-2, we can see that we have a list of four items, and it will be better to convert the list with the ID list1 to a listview. I know you are thinking: add a data-role="listview" to the ul. But that will not work. And that is because the page was already loaded and our list was not detected as a list view widget in the first term.

To create a widget dynamically we have to call the widget constructor. Every widget has its own constructor and it's just a jQuery function with the widget name, so if we execute $("#list1").listview(), the ul will be converted and rendered as a list view widget immediately (Figure 6-3).

If we have a list of a elements we want to convert to buttons, we just call:

```
$("a").button();
```

Or if we are creating one dynamically:

```
var button = $("<a>").attr("href", "somewhere.html").button();
```

Updating Widgets

Now we know how to create jQuery Mobile widgets dynamically. But what happens if the widget is already created and rendered and we are just changing its content? For example, we are adding items to a list view, or we are changing the value of a checkbox.

In these cases, we need to refresh the widget. To do that we need to call the widget function with the string refresh as an argument, for example:

```
$("#list1").listview('refresh');
$("#checkbox").val('true').checkboxradio('refresh');
```

Going back to our last sample, if we initially define our list1 as an empty listview, we need to refresh the widget after adding the list elements. If not, the list elements will not have the right rendering for the user interface:

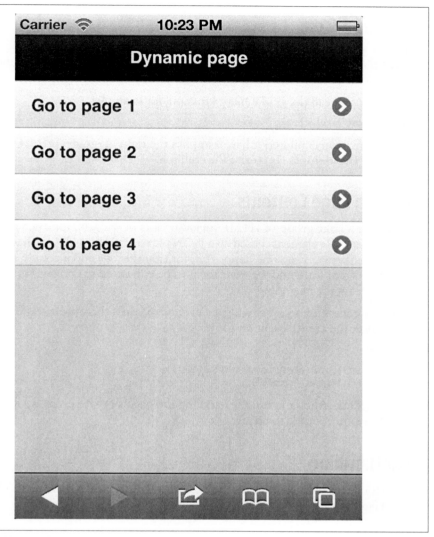

Figure 6-3. Using widget constructors, we can create every widget dynamically—in this case, we create a list view

```
<ul id="list1">
</ul>
```

After adding items, we call:

```
$("#list1").listview('refresh');
```

Creating Grids

There is a special widget that we can use to create CSS grids, as we have seen in a previous chapter. To do so, we need to use an HTML element with children and convert it to a grid of *n* columns based on the number of children.

To use it, we just call the `grid` jQuery function, for example:

```
$("#element").grid();
```

Based on how many children it has, it applies the right `ui-grid-<letter>` class to the element and the `ui-block-letter` to the children.

Changing Page Contents

If we change a large group of HTML including lots of widgets, for example, creating various `collapsible` elements based on a JSON file received by AJAX, we have to refresh the whole container. The same happens if, for example, we add a couple of `input` elements to a current form and we want them to be converted to widgets, as if they were in the page from the beginning.

To refresh a container, so every widget can check again if there are instances to create, we can trigger the `create` event on the page.

For example:

```
$("#content").html(newHTMLcontentWithWidgets);
$("#page1").trigger("create");
```

Every widget constructor is usually handling the page's `create` event, so it will detect again if there are controls to create.

Event Handling

jQuery Mobile provides new events available using the typical jQuery methods such as `bind` or `live`.

Page Events

We are used to normal HTML page events, such as `load` and `DOMready` events applied by the browser for each HTTP page loaded in the current session. In a jQuery Mobile framework, we have different elements where we apply events. As we already know, a jQuery Mobile document will have different pages (internal or loaded externally), so we need to think in terms of jQuery Mobile pages for loading.

Every page (element with `data-role="page"`) has a set of different events that we can handle globally (for all the pages at the same time) or singly for an individual page.

To handle page events globally, we can call `$(document).bind` or to be more specific `$(":jqmData(role='page')").bind`. We can also use `live` instead of `bind` to allow binding to future pages to be added to the DOM in the future.

Every page has creation, loading, and showing events.

Creation events

Every page has its own creation or initialization events. The events available are:

`pagebeforecreate`
> After the page is inserted in the DOM and before its widgets are created.

`pagecreate`
> After the page is created but before widgets are rendered.

`pageinit`
> After the page is fully loaded. This should be the most used event for a page.

`pageremove`
> After the page was removed from the DOM (usually when it was an AJAX-loaded page that is not currently the active page).

For example, we can bind a `pageinit` event using the jQuery `live` method:

```
$("#page2").live("pageinit", function(event) {

});
```

 Remember that to use `bind`, the element must be present in the DOM at the time of the binding. If it's not available, we can use `live` instead. jQuery 1.7 supports a new "on" function that is not available when using jQuery Mobile 1.0 and jQuery 1.6.4.

Loading events

Not every page is loaded by default with the first jQuery Mobile document. For every page loaded using AJAX, we have special event handlers that usually are bound to `$(document)` because the pages are not in the DOM yet to bind the handler to.

The available loading events are:

`pagebeforeload`
> Executed before any AJAX request is done

`pageload`
> Executed after the page was loaded and inserted into the DOM

`pageloadfailed`
> Executed when the page could not be loaded

Every one of these events handlers will receive two arguments: an event object and a data object.

The first parameter will have typical event handler values, as well as methods such as preventDefault() that will prevent default behavior. Using this idea, we can force the framework to not show the default error message alert and provide our own UI:

```
$(document).bind("pageloadfailed", function(event, data) {
    data.preventDefault();
    // Custom error management
});
```

The second argument is an object containing different attributes, including:

url
:   Absolute or relative URL as it was requested by $.mobile.loadPage.

absUrl
:   Absolute URL.

dataUrl
:   The URL to be used as the page identifier.

options
:   All the options passed to $.mobile.loadPage, for example to know if it was a get or post request.

xhr
:   The XMLHttpRequest object for low-level management.

textStatus
:   Used for error message.

errorThrown
:   Error exception object, valid only on pageloadfailed.

deferred
:   Valid only on pagebeforeload and pageloadfailed and only when we call event.preventDefault(). In these cases, we must call the resolve() or reject() methods of this object so the frameworks knows how to handle the situation.

 If you want to handle page initialization, you should avoid using load, ready, or even mobileinit. The right event is pageinit and is available for every page. If you are binding it inside mobileinit, use live instead of bind.

Showing events

A page can be initialized once but shown many times, because the user can go forward and backwards. That is why we can handle showing and hiding events over pages.

These events are divided into change page events and transition events.

The available change page events are:

pagebeforechange
    Executed before the change is made and before any transition begins

pagechange
    Executed after the change is done

pagechangefailed
    Executed if the change could not be done

Every event handler will receive two arguments:

toPage
    A string with the URL of the destination page or a DOM object with the destination page if it's an internal page change

options
    The same options sent to `$.mobile.changePage`

The available transition events are:

pagebeforeshow
    Executed before the page is going to be shown on screen using a transition (the page is still hidden)

pageshow
    Executed after the page was transitioned in and is currently on screen

pagebeforehide
    Executed before the page is hidden (while the page is still visible)

pagehide
    Executed after the page has transitioned out and is currently hidden

Every event handler for transition events will receive one argument, being a DOM jQuery object of the related page. If it's a show event, you will receive the previous page object; and if it's a hide event, you will receive the next page object.

Widget Events

Every widget that shows/hides content dynamically, such as `collapsible`, triggers an `updatelayout` event because the page layout has been changed. We may want to handle it to update some other thing on the UI.

Orientation Event

A mobile device can be moved and it can have at least two orientations: portrait and landscape. We may want to change some appearance or behavior when the orientation is changed, so jQuery Mobile provides us a `orientationchange` event that can be attached to the document.

This event is currently linked to resize on some platforms where native orientation change is not supported. On some platforms, when the orientationchange event is fired, the window frame is still old, so you will not get the right width/height values. If you want to force this event to refresh when the values are updated, you can execute $.mobile.orientationChangeEnabled=false.

The event handler will receive a string as the first argument with the values portrait or landscape. This value is always the right one on every platform (it doesn't have the width/height problem):

```
$(document).bind("orientationchange", function(orientation) {
    if (orientation=="landscape") {
        // We are now in landscape
    } else {
        // We are now in portrait
    }
});
```

Gesture Events

jQuery Mobile offers us some gesture touch events that we can bind to any DOM element. The gesture events offered in jQuery Mobile 1.0 includes:

tap
> Executed after a quick touch on the screen.

taphold
> Executed when the user touches the screen and maintains it pressed for one second. Useful for showing contextual menus.

swipeleft
> Executed when the user swipes a finger from right to left.

swiperight
> Executed when the user swipes a finger from left to right.

The next example will bind a swiperight event to a page to go back:

```
$(document).bind("mobileinit", function() {
    $("#page2").live("swiperight", goBackToPage1);
});

function goBackToPage1() {
    $.mobile.changePage("#page1", { reverse: true });
    $("#page2").unbind("swiperight", goBackToPage1);
}
```

Virtual Clicks Events

Virtual click? That sounds strange, right? Let's talk about it for a minute. Most mobile touch web browsers have a delay of 300–500 milliseconds when you are using click events (such as `click`, `mouseover`) and this delay is not there when you are using touch events (such as `touchstart`, `touchmove`). The other problem is that not every touch browser supports touch events.

Virtual click events are wrappers that we can use instead of touch or click events and they will choose the right one depending on the platform you are running. It also normalizes position information and can be used only for single touch (not multi-touch).

Virtual click events can be used exactly the same as the click events, but the event name has a `v` prefix. The framework includes: `vclick`, `vmouseover`, `vmousedown`, `vmousemove`, `vmouseup`, and `vmousecancel`.

## CHAPTER 7

Creating Themes

jQuery Mobile allows us to customize the entire user interface through themes and CSS. We need to remember that jQuery Mobile generates HTML and CSS so every feature can be overridden using CSS.

In Figure 7-1, we can see some jQuery Mobile websites with different user interfaces. If you want to see more of these customized UI websites, you can check *http://jqmgallery .com*.

Figure 7-1. The site shows hundreds of mobile webapps created using jQuery Mobile, including some with a nice UI that looks really different than the standard theme

A theme is a set of color swatches defining:

- Text colors
- Background colors and gradients
- Font

We can define up to 26 color swatches, from **a** to **z**, while typically we will have at least five different color swatches.

A theme also has a global definition that applies to every swatch color, including:

- Text and box effects, such as shadows and rounded corners
- Active state for buttons and other controls

The idea of a global definition is to maintain the same experience not matter which swatch color is applied. For example, in the default theme a selected button is always blue, not matter which color swatch is used for that button.

A theme is stored in a CSS file that is included in our HTML file with the structural CSS file provided by the framework. The structural CSS file should not be modified, as this could cause problems with future versions. If we want to override some behaviors defined in the structural CSS, the preferred way is to define them in another CSS file that will be loaded after the structural one (therefore, it will override the style's definitions).

 A theme should not define size or position for elements. That behavior is defined in the structural file, and we should not change it unless we know what we are doing.

ThemeRoller

The easiest way to create a theme is to use the online free tool ThemeRoller available at *http://jquerymobile.com/themeroller*. As we can see in Figure 7-2, the ThemeRoller allows us to define the color of every element in the web page using the inspector panel at the right or with drag-and-drop gestures.

The utility interface is divided into three panes:

- Swatch color selector at the left
- Palette pane at the top
- Preview pane at the right

If you drag a color from the palette pane and drop it over the preview pane over a background or a text snippet, it will automatically be applied to that style.

 You can move the lightness and saturation sliders to get more colors in the palette.

Figure 7-2. The ThemeRoller on a desktop browser

Global Settings

In the Global settings tab (as in Figure 7-3) at the right we can define:

- Font family
- Active state for buttons and other controls
- Corner radius for control groups and buttons
- Icon properties
- Box shadow

Swatch Color Settings

We can also change the tab and select one of the letters—each one representing a color swatch (Figure 7-4). Every color swatch can be customized with:

- Header/footer bar color, shadow, and background
- Content body colors and borders
- Button colors and borders in normal, hover, and pressed states

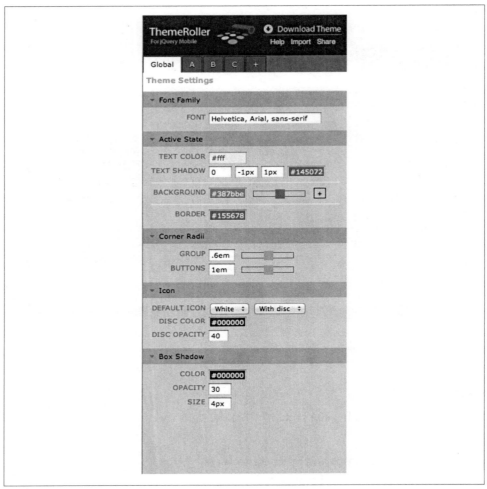

Figure 7-3. The Global settings tab

Using the + tab we can add new color swatches to the theme.

When you are defining a background color you will see a little slider. If you move that slider you are changing the gradient, and you will have a live preview at the right. If you click on the little plus icon to the right of the slider, you will get a deeper gradient configuration.

Inspector

If you turn on the inspector with the push button at the top, you can click in the preview pane over an element and the properties for that element will open on the left side.

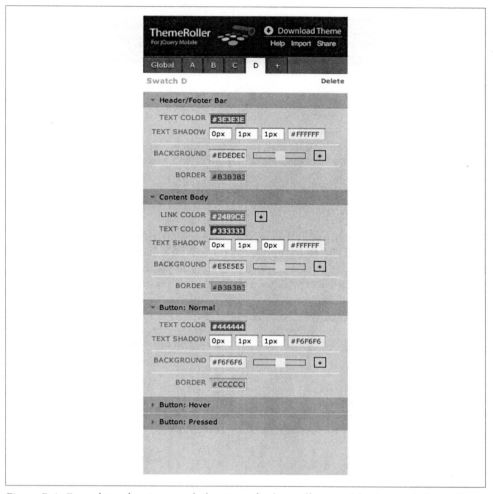

Figure 7-4. Every letter has its own declaration of colors, effects, and backgrounds for toolbars, content, and buttons

Adobe Kuler

Adobe Kuler is a service-based community from Adobe for color palettes. People share their favorite color palettes on the system and we can browse through them on the website *http://kuler.adobe.com* or inside any Creative Suite application.

jQuery Mobile ThemeRoller includes a Kuler widget (seen in Figure 7-5) that allows us to browse and search thousands of color palettes on the network and use those colors to drag and drop over the preview pane.

Figure 7-5. The Adobe Kuler widget can be opened at the top of ThemeRoller to search for great color palettes on the Web

 If you have an image, for example your website logo, and you want to get the palette color from that, you can create a palette from your image at *http://kuler.adobe.com*, make it public, and search for it in the ThemeRoller.

Exporting Your Theme

When you are done designing your theme, you can export it using the Download Theme button at the top right of the web interface. You will be asked for a theme name (see Figure 7-6) and you will get a code snippet to copy and paste to use your new theme. If you press Download Zip, you will get a ZIP file with your theme CSS file inside—minimized and ready for debugging.

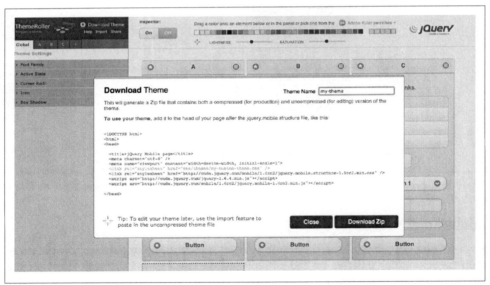

Figure 7-6. Exporting a theme is as simple as defining a name and downloading a ZIP file

You can also import a theme into ThemeRoller to be changed easily on the web interface. Just use the Import option and copy/paste your CSS theme file inside.

Fireworks Theme Editor

If you are a user of Adobe Fireworks, you have the jQuery Mobile Theme editor at your disposal. If you have version CS5.1, you can download the free plug-in: "Fireworks CSS3 Mobile Pack" from *http://labs.adobe.com*.

When you have the pack installed, open Fireworks and select Commands → jQuery Mobile → Create New Theme. You will get a new image that looks like Figure 7-7.

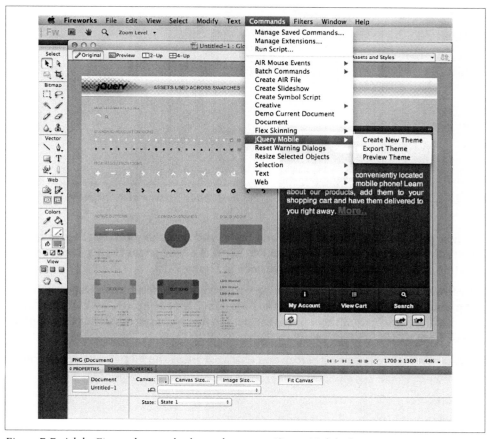

Figure 7-7. Adobe Fireworks can also be used to create jQuery Mobile themes

If you don't have Adobe Fireworks, you can download a 30-day trial version from *http://adobe.com/go/fireworks*.

This image acts like a template that we can change, while maintaining the same instance names. The image is divided into six pages that we can see upon opening the Pages panel (Windows → Pages), as we can see in Figure 7-8.

Figure 7-8. If you open the Pages panel, you will find the general designer and one page per color swatch

The first page is called Global Assets and Styles and includes global styling and icons for all color swatches, as seen in Figure 7-9. Then, we have pages from a to e for which to define and change color swatches, as seen in Figure 7-10.

We can add more swatches by duplicating a page (right-click and select Duplicate Page) and providing the right letter name in the Page panel, for example f. We can also delete swatches if we don't want them in the theme, but it is recommended that we maintain at least from a to c.

We can select any element on screen and change it using the Fireworks user interface, including:

- Text color
- Background (plain color or linear gradient)
- Font style and size
- Shadow filter
- Opacity (transparency)

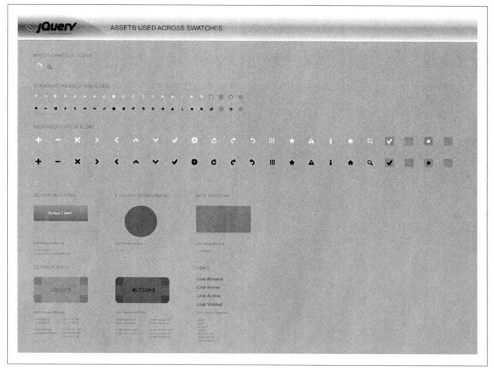

Figure 7-9. The global configuration page allows us to change icons and global settings

On the global assets page, we can define:

- Icons: low- and high-resolution icons. We can change these icons as long as we maintain the instance name, for example `ui-icon-plus` for the plus sign.
- Active button style.
- Icon background: we can change its opacity.
- Box shadow: we can change color and shape of the shadow.
- Corner radius for control groups and for buttons: every corner can be changed by selecting it and using the Properties panel to define its roundness.
- Links in all states: normal, hover, active, and visited.

On every swatch color page, we can define:

- Header and footer areas
- Content area
- Buttons in all states: normal, hover and down

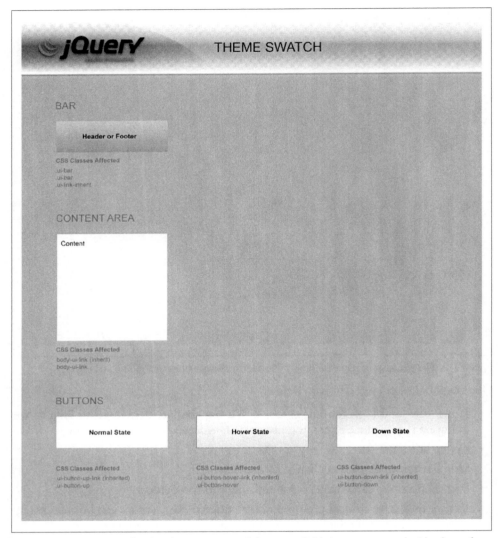

Figure 7-10. Every swatch color that we want to define is available in a page named with a letter from a to z

When we are done making changes, we can preview the theme file using Commands → jQuery Mobile → Preview Theme. If we like the theme, we can export it using Commands → jQuery Mobile → Export Theme.

We can keep the jQuery Mobile Preview panel open using Windows → Extensions → jQuery Mobile Theme Preview as seen in Figure 7-11. If we change the swatch (changing the current page), we must refresh the Preview panel to see it applied.

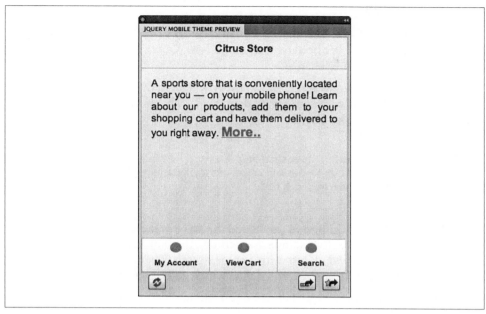

Figure 7-11. We can open the jQuery Mobile Theme Preview and see how our theme will look on a real webapp

 If we only want to change the icon images and not the CSS file, on the jQuery Mobile Theme Preview panel, we can find an icon to Export Sprite Images.

Fireworks will export the designs to CSS3, including gradients (with prefixes for all the browsers) and include a big image with all the icons to be used by the framework as a CSS Sprite. We will need to provide a folder and a theme name for the export action. We will get one CSS file and an images folder ready to include in our project.

It's a good practice to save the file as a Fireworks PNG file so we can use it in the future to make small changes in the theme without starting from scratch.

 If we are using our own theme CSS file, we need to use the structural CSS file in our webapp and not the CSS file that includes the default theme.

Editing Themes

The theme is just a CSS file. That means we can create the CSS file from scratch or edit one using any text editor. We need to understand how jQuery Mobile defines elements and classes to know what to change.

jQuery Mobile uses classes to define styles. Every widget in the HTML markup will be converted to an element with some class definitions. Therefore, our UI work will be just defining styles for these classes.

 Remember that in the content area of a page, we can have any HTML that we want, so we can still create our own markup with CSS styles apart from the framework CSS.

Every class is defined including a `ui` prefix and the color swatch as a suffix, `ui-<name>-<color-swatch>`. Therefore, for example for defining the buttons, the class name is `ui-btn-a` for a color swatch and `ui-btn-c` for c color swatch. Then, from the HTML using `data-theme` or another attribute we will define which color swatch will be applied.

Table 7-1 shows the typical class names we can edit and define in a theme CSS file.

Table 7-1. Classes that we can define in the theme file to customize the UI (<x> defines the color swatch)

Class name	Description
`ui-bar-<x>`	Headers, footers, and other bars
`ui-btn-up-<x>`	Buttons in normal state
`ui-btn-hover-<x>`	Buttons in hover state
`ui-btn-down-<x>`	Buttons in pressed state
`ui-btn-active`	Buttons in active state (all swatch colors)
`ui-body-<x>`	Page body
`ui-link-<x>`	Links
`ui-icon-<x>`	Icon for buttons and other widgets
`ui-corner-all`	Applies to all the controls that have rounded corners
`ui-corner-<tl/tr/bl/br>`	Applies to top left/top right/bottom left/bottom right rounded corners
`ui-corner-<top/bottom>`	Applies to the top/bottom rounded corners
`ui-corner-<left/right>`	Applies to the left/right rounded corners
`ui-shadow`	Applies to any element that can use shadow
`ui-disabled`	Applies to any element that is disabled using HTML

If we want to provide, for example, a different UI for the header and the footer (both using the same class ui-bar), we should change the color swatch that each toolbar is using from the markup.

Custom Transitions

We can create our own transitions using JavaScript (as seen in the previous chapter) or by applying pure CSS3. If we are going to use CSS3 animations, we need to understand how they work.

If we define a data-transition that the system doesn't know, it looks to see if there is a JavaScript handler for that name. If not, it tries to apply a CSS3 animation.

The transition name is used as a class name applied both to the current page and the next one. The in class is also applied to the next page and the out class is applied to the current page.

That means that if we define a transition called card, we should define a selector for .card.in and .card.out. Optionally, we can define the reverse transition that will be used when going back and the reverse class is also added, so .card.in.reverse and .card.out.reverse should also be defined.

We don't need to provide animation timing functions nor duration because these are already defined in the global CSS structural file.

Using CSS3 animations, we can create our own transition. Our card transition will be similar to slide, but the idea is that all the pages are placed one over the other, and when we go to the next card we just remove the one at the top (current page) and the other is revealed at the back (without animation):

```
.card.out {
    -webkit-transform: translateY(-100%);
    -webkit-animation-name: cardout;
    z-index: 1; /* It's above */
}

.card.in {
    -webkit-transform: translateY(0);
    z-index: 0; /* It's below */
}

@-webkit-keyframes cardout {
    from {
        -webkit-transform: translateY(0%);
    }
```

```
    to {
        -webkit-transform: translateY(-100%);
    }
}
```

We can add this declaration to our theme CSS file or to another CSS file. To use this transition, we just define it using `data-transition` or JavaScript:

```
<a href="#page2" data-role="button" data-transition="card">Page 2</a>
```

If we want this animation to work on Firefox for Android, Opera, or Internet Explorer 10, we should provide alternatives with their own prefixes, `-moz`, `-o`, and `-ms`.

## CHAPTER 8

Installation and Offline Access

Using HTML5 and some other extensions, we can enable our jQuery Mobile application to work totally offline as if it were installed in the mobile device as a native app.

We can also package our jQuery Mobile webapp as a native app for store distribution, but that is for a later chapter. In this chapter we are creating an offline experience of our webapp without store distribution.

With this solution, the user can access our webapp from the mobile browser and then install it on her device. That means that next time she accesses the same webapp through the same URL or through an application icon, it will load from the local repository and not from our server.

Package Definition

The first thing to do is to define our package. To do that we are going to use an HTML5 API called Application Cache also known as Offline API available in the W3C draft.

This API does not currently work on every mobile browser but its compatibility includes most tablets and smartphones. You can check current compatibility of this API at *http://mobilehtml5.org*.

Our first step is to define what we want. Do we want a full offline application? Do we want some pages or data to be updated from the server every time? Do we want to have a local data cache and, if we have online access, update it?

The second step is to define the package. The package is a list of files that must be downloaded by the browser when the user accesses our website. This list must include every JavaScript, CSS, image, or resource that we want to access offline. As we are creating a jQuery Mobile application, we need to add to this package all the jQuery Mobile files, including CSS structural, theme, images, and JavaScript files.

HTML Manifest

The package list is delivered through a text file known as a cache manifest. This file must have a first line with the literal text CACHE MANIFEST and then a list of URLs—relative or absolute—of every resource to download to the device.

The main HTML file is implicit in the package, so we don't need to add it on the manifest.

It doesn't matter if all the files defined are in the same server or not. This means that we can always link the jQuery Mobile CDN for the framework files.

The manifest file supports comment lines if they start with #.

 If any file of the manifest failed to download while installing the package, then the entire package is invalidated. That means that if we are defining resources on third-party servers, we will rely on these servers for our app to be installed.

For example, a typical jQuery Mobile application's manifest with one document (no external pages), should look like:

```
CACHE MANIFEST:

# jQuery core
http://code.jquery.com/jquery-1.6.1.min.js

# jQuery Mobile files without custom theme
http://code.jquery.com/mobile/1.0/jquery.mobile-1.0.min.css
http://code.jquery.com/mobile/1.0/jquery.mobile-1.0.min.js
http://code.jquery.com/mobile/1.0/images/ajax-loader.png
http://code.jquery.com/mobile/1.0/images/icons-18-black.png
http://code.jquery.com/mobile/1.0/images/icons-18-white.png
http://code.jquery.com/mobile/1.0/images/icons-36-black.png
http://code.jquery.com/mobile/1.0/images/icons-36-white.png

# My app files, relative to the HTML document
images/logo.png
data/countries.json
```

This file usually is stored under the name *offline.appcache* and must be served using the MIME type text/cache-manifest to work properly. You should contact your server's administrator if you don't know how to set up this MIME type.

If your server supports PHP, you can just change the file's extension to PHP and use this template and it will work without any special configuration:

```
<?php header('Content-Type: text/cache-manifest');
?>CACHE MANIFEST:
```

The next step is to define in our HTML the URL of the manifest file. This is done using the new HTML5 manifest attribute in the html element.

```
<html manifest="offline.appcache">
      <-- Rest of our webapp -->
</html>
```

Download Process

When a compatible browsers finds a manifest declaration, it downloads the manifest file in the background and if it's a valid file delivered with the valid MIME type, it starts the webapp download process.

This background process is completely separate from the normal page load. The background process downloads every file in the manifest and it stores them locally in a private place.

 If only one manifest's resource can't be downloaded (it doesn't exist, the server is down, etc.), the entire package is invalidated and nothing is stored locally.

If the package is installed successfully, the next time the user accesses the same URL, the browser will load the local version instead of looking for the server's version. The browser will automatically enters an offline state, even if the user is online. That means that, by default, we can't access any other online resource not declared previously in the manifest file.

If the package was not installed successfully, then the next time, the page will load again from the web server. The reasons for not installing a package can be:

- The manifest file was not valid, doesn't exist, or it has a wrong MIME type.
- At least one of the resources in the manifest couldn't be accessed.
- The user exited the browser or the web page before all the resources were properly downloaded.

Using a debugging tool we can see what the package contains. For iOS Simulator, you can download the free tool iWebInspector (*http://iwebinspector.com*) and you will find the application cache information in the Resources tab, as seen in Figure 8-1.

 To access local resources downloaded by the application cache we shouldn't change our code. We just access the resource as if it were online, using the same relative or absolute URL we define in the manifest. The browser is smart enough to load the local version of that file.

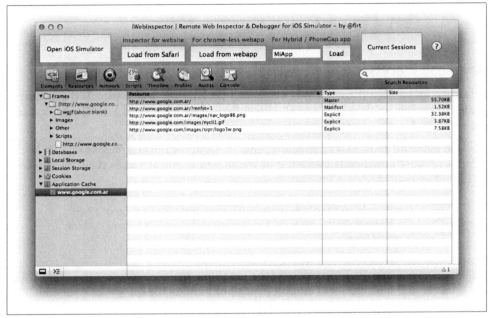

Figure 8-1. Here we can see the Resources tab of iWebInspector showing the application cache package contents

Accessing Online Resources

If we access any resource that was not originally defined in the manifest file, then the process will fail because our application is sandboxed offline. If we know for sure that we are going to need some information from the Web, we can define it in the manifest file in a special section called `NETWORK:`. By default, all the resources are declared in an implicit `CACHE:` section. A section is just a line ending with a colon. So, if we want our *countries.json* file to always be delivered from the server, we can change our manifest to:

```
CACHE MANIFEST:

# jQuery core
http://code.jquery.com/jquery-1.6.1.min.js

# jQuery Mobile files without custom theme
http://code.jquery.com/mobile/1.0/jquery.mobile-1.0.min.css
http://code.jquery.com/mobile/1.0/jquery.mobile-1.0.min.js
http://code.jquery.com/mobile/1.0/images/ajax-loader.png
http://code.jquery.com/mobile/1.0/images/icons-18-black.png
http://code.jquery.com/mobile/1.0/images/icons-18-white.png
http://code.jquery.com/mobile/1.0/images/icons-36-black.png
http://code.jquery.com/mobile/1.0/images/icons-36-white.png

# My app files, relative to the HTML document
images/logo.png
```

```
# Resources that should be downloaded from the web
NETWORK:
data/countries.json
```

Then, *countries.json* will not be downloaded with the resources and will be accessed online every time. If there is no Internet connection, we will not get this file, unless the browser has a cached version (using the typical web cache, not the application cache).

 If the browser supports this Offline API then we have two new events available that we can handle on the document: online and offline. And we can query the browser to see whether we have an Internet connection or not via window.onLine Boolean property.

In the network section, we can use wildcards, such as * or folders, and every resource in that folder will be accessible from the Web while we are in an offline operation.

So if we want to have an offline application that can access the full Web if the user has a connection, then we can just use:

```
NETWORK:
*
```

With the previous sample only the files before NETWORK: will be loaded from the offline package, and every other resource will be loaded from the Web.

 The manifest file also supports a FALLBACK: section that is beyond the scope of this book where we can define alternative URLs for network resources if there is no Internet connection.

Updating Resources

We've said that when the package is installed all the resources—including the main HTML document—will always be loaded from the local storage and not from the Web. Therefore, it's fair to ask: how can we update a resource? What happens if we want to update the theme CSS file, change an image, or add a new page link in the HTML document?

Well, I've got to admit that I lie a bit. Or did I omit something? I'm not sure if it was a lie, but it was definitely an omission. When the user opens our webapp for the second time—and later times—while the app is always loaded from the local storage, in the background the browser tries to get an updated manifest file from the server.

If there is no Internet connection, nothing happens and the user always has the local version. If there is a network connection available, then the browser compares the new manifest file recently downloaded from the server with the local version it has from the original webapp download. It makes a byte-by-byte comparison on the two files. If one byte changed, then the whole manifest is invalidated and every resource is downloaded again using the new manifest file.

Go back to the previous paragraph and read it again. Done? OK, let's try to check again what is happening. If we change a CSS file and the CSS name is the same, the manifest will be the same so we won't have any update on the downloaded files. We need to change the manifest for the webapp to receive the update.

Changing the manifest when we make an update can involve adding a space, changing the resource name (versioning it), or even having a comment line with a random value or the last modified date, for example:

```
CACHE MANIFEST
# webapp updated 2012-01-01
```

If we change a byte—for example, the date—the whole manifest will be invalidated and the platform will download all the files again. Yes, all the files. With this API we can't update just one resource.

 Using a mix of the Application Cache and the Web Storage API, we can create a mechanism to download resources—such as CSS, JavaScript, or images—and store them locally without reloading the whole webapp.

There another unpleasant problem when dealing with manifest updates: if there is an update, the platform downloads all the resources in the manifest again. However, this download process is done in the background while the previous files are on the screen. So if there is an update, the user receives the previous version until she reloads the application. Next time, the installed package has changed, so it will load the new resources.

That means that if we change the manifest, the user must load the page twice to use the new version. We can use events to handle this situation.

JavaScript Object

There is a global JavaScript object that helps us to know the status of the application cache. The object is applicationCache and it has a status property that can have one of the values listed in Table 8-1.

To be compatible with all the browsers, we should always check first to see if the object is available:

```
if (window.applicationCache!=undefined) {
    // The API is available
}
```

Table 8-1. Values that can have the applicationCache.status property

Value	Constant	Description
0	UNCACHED	This is the first load of the page, or no manifest file is available.
1	IDLE	The cache is idle.
2	CHECKING	The local manifest file is being checked against the server's manifest file.
3	DOWNLOADING	The resources are being downloaded (first time or update).
4	UPDATEREADY	There is an update that was downloaded but it will be available on next load.

We can use constants to ask about the current status, for example:

```
if (window.applicationCache!=undefined) {
    // The API is available
    if (applicationCache.status==applicationCache.UPDATEREADY) {
        // There is an update waiting for reload
    }
}
```

The `applicationCache` object has the methods `update()`, which will force an update check and `swapCache()`, which will swap from the old resources cache to the new one (if a new one was already downloaded). However, the HTML document and the resources already loaded will not be there until we make a full reload with `history.reload()`.

Events

The `applicationCache` object has events that we can handle to manage every situation. For example if the user is accessing our website for the first time, we can show a "Downloading app" message while the resources are downloaded so the user will wait, increasing the probability of a complete download.

The possible events that we can bind to are listed in Table 8-2.

Table 8-2. Events that we can handle using the applicationCache object

Event name	Fired when
checking	The browser is checking the manifest.
downloading	The browser starts to download the resources on the manifest.
progress	One resource was downloaded (fired for every resource, so we can create a progress bar).
cached	The first download process has finished properly.
noupdate	The manifest was compared with the server and no update is available.
updateready	There was an update and the new resources were downloaded properly and waiting for a reload.
error	There was an error downloading a resource.
obsolete	When checking an update, the manifest is no longer valid, so the webapp was deleted from the storage and will not be offline next time.

On a typical situation we are going to:

- Capture downloading so we can show a message to the user and optionally an animated spinner
- Capture progress to make a progress bar, as seen in Figure 8-2
- Capture cached to hide the loading message and tell the user that the app was installed
- Capture error to hide the loading message and tell the user about the situation
- Capture updateready to inform the user that there is an update ready and ask the user if she wants to reload now to access the updated app

We can bind to this events using addEventListener, for example:

```
if (window.applicationCache!=undefined) {
    // The API is available
    applicationCache.addEventListener('updateready', function() {
        // There is an update waiting for reload
        if (confirm("There is an update ready. Do you want to load it now?")) {
            history.reload();
        }
    });
}
```

Figure 8-2. Here we can see the Financial Times iPad application being downloaded (app.ft.com)

Icon Installation

When the application is downloaded using the application cache, we can invite the user to add an icon to the home screen or application's menu. This will allow the user to open our webapp from a shortcut icon instead of typing the URL again. Even for a normal user, the idea of opening an offline application—one that can be used on a plane—through the browser after typing a URL is strange.

The user can add an icon even if there is no manifest. In that case, the icon will be just a shortcut to the online version of our webapp.

> The application can also invite the user to add our webapp to bookmarks. However, in the mobile space, it's more common to use installed icons instead of bookmarks for a typical user.

No platform allows an automatic icon installation, so we need to invite the user to install our webapp, providing the instructions on screen.

Invitation

We can invite the user to add the app to the home screen in different ways. For example, YouTube, Google Maps, and Facebook on iOS invite the user with a floating `div` that looks like Figure 8-3.

Usually we are going to store a cookie or an HTML5 `localStorage` value to know if we've already invited the user so the user will see the invitation only once.

Icon Name

The icon will have a name inside the home screen menu on some platforms (as seen in Figure 8-4) or inside the applications menu on some other platforms (as seen in Figure 8-5). The name below the icon is by default defined by the `title` HTML element. That means that if we are going to invite the user to install the icon, we should always use a very short title (one or two words) that can fit in the area.

> In a jQuery Mobile document, if the user adds the webapp to the home screen or application's menu while not in the first page (external or internal), the shortcut will point to the active page and not the home page, and that page's `data-title` will be used.

In Figure 8-6 we can see how the user can add our website to the home screen on different platforms.

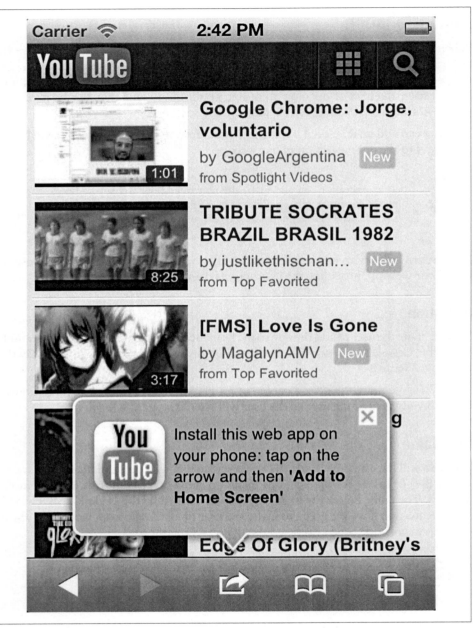

Figure 8-3. Many mobile websites invite the user to add an icon to the home page via a balloon

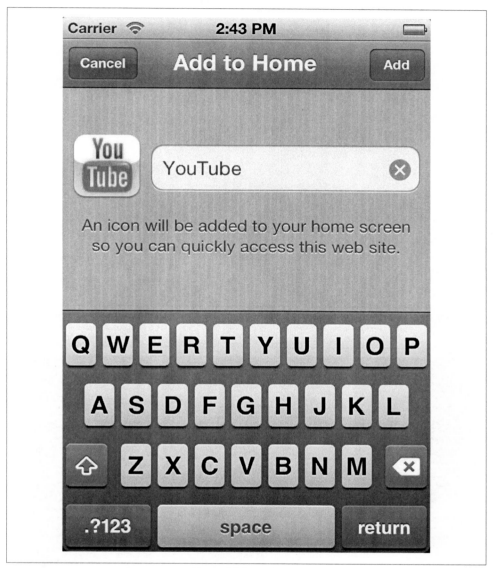

Figure 8-4. On iOS, the user can add an icon to the home screen

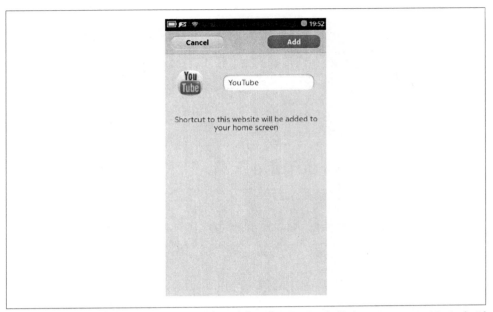

Figure 8-5. The Nokia N9 also allows the user to add an icon to the home screen, as with Android and iPhone

Figure 8-6. Here you can see many platforms and the menus to add the page to the home screen or applications menu

Icon Definition

In typical web pages, the only icon definition is done using the classic `favicon` `link` element that usually is done using `rel="icon"` and also `rel="shortcut icon"` to be compatible for all browsers:

```
<link rel="icon" type="image/png" href="favicon.png" />
<link rel="shortcut icon" type="image/png" href="favicon.png" />
```

The problem with this icon is that it originally used ICO format (a 16×16 bitmap image) and now it supports other formats, such as PNG, but they are usually small (maximum 32×32 pixels), so they are small compared to the sizes of the icons on a smartphone or tablet home screen icon. That is why usually these icons are not used or if they are used, they are just at a corner of the real icon.

 If a platform is not compatible with home screen icons, we can always package our jQuery Mobile webapp in a hybrid application—such as by using PhoneGap—and distribute it as a native app on our website or in stores as we'll see in later chapters.

There is no other standard for icon definition. However, Apple for iOS invented a `meta` tag for their own icons that can be used now for other platforms, such as Android Browser and MeeGo 1.2 (Nokia N9's Browser). We should provide as many icons as we can. Every platform will take only the one it supports. If a platform doesn't support any icon, usually they use an standard shortcut icon or a screenshot of the upper-left part of the website—usually our logo.

The Apple de facto standard is also a `link` tag with a `rel="apple-touch-icon"` or a `rel="apple-touch-icon-precomposed"` and an optional `sizes` attribute.

Apple, by default, applies rounded corners, a shadow and a 3D glow effect to every icon defined with `rel="apple-touch-icon"`. If we don't want a shadow and 3D glow effect (useful for transparent icons), we can use `rel="apple-touch-icon-precomposed"` instead.

Android Browser supports only `rel="apple-touch-icon-precomposed"`, as it doesn't add any effect to the icon.

We can provide icons in different sizes for different platforms. If we provide only one icon, it will be resized for every platform, and the results may not be good. We can have different `link` elements with different sizes using the `sizes` attribute, for example, `sizes="57x57"`. The preferred format is always PNG.

The available sizes are shown in Table 8-3.

Table 8-3. Icon sizes available for home screen icons

Platform	Size	rel	Sizes attribute
iPhone 3, 3GS iPod Touch 1-3	57×57	apple-touch-icon and apple-touch-icon-precomposed	Yes from 4.2
iPhone 4, 4S, iPod Touch 4	114×114	apple-touch-icon and apple-touch-icon-precomposed	Yes from 4.2
iPad 1, 2	72×72	apple-touch-icon and apple-touch-icon-precomposed	Yes from 4.2
Android Browser	Any size	apple-touch-icon-precomposed	No
Nokia N9 Browser	80×80	apple-touch-icon	Yes

Android Browser doesn't support the sizes attribute, so it will ignore it. If we define several icons, Android will use the last precomposed one. If we want iOS to ignore the Android tag, the hack is to provide an invalid sizes attribute, for example: sizes="android-only".

 iOS devices 4.2 or below don't understand the sizes attributes, so if we declare different icon sizes, the latest one will be used. So it's a good practice to use the lower size icon below.

Therefore, to provide all the possible icons, we can use the following code on the head element and save your icon in every size:

```
<link rel="icon" href="icons/icon32.png">
<link rel="shortcut icon" href="icons/icon32.png">

<link rel="apple-touch-icon" href="icons/icon57.png" sizes="57x57">
<link rel="apple-touch-icon" href="icons/icon114.png" sizes="114x114">
<link rel="apple-touch-icon" href="icons/icon72.png" sizes="72x72">
<link rel="apple-touch-icon" sizes="80x80" href="icons/icon80.png">
<link rel="apple-touch-icon-precomposed" sizes="android-only" href="icons/icon57.png">
```

In Figure 8-7 we can see our icon applied in the home screen of different platforms.

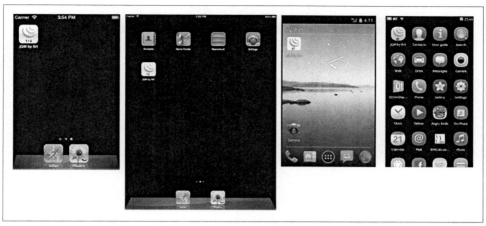

Figure 8-7. The same icon with different sizes applied in different platforms' home or applications screens

Full Screen

On iOS-only, including iPhone and iPad, we can go further with our webapp. We can create a chrome-less, full-screen webapp without any Safari controls (neither address bar nor toolbar). This will only works when the user opens the app from the home screen and if we define the following `meta` tag in the HTML page:

```
<meta name="apple-mobile-web-app-capable"
    content="yes">
```

Then, when we open the page, it's completely full screen, so we need to provide back buttons explicitly on the user interface as seen in Figure 8-8.

Detecting Full Screen

If we are on iOS, we can force the full-screen usage of our webapp using the `naviga` `tor.standalone` property. If this property is available, it can be `false`, meaning that the user is on Safari, or `true` if our webapp was opened from the home screen icon.

With that idea, we can force installation and usage through a full-screen webapp. While installed, there is no visual difference for the user between a native app downloaded from the AppStore and our chrome-less webapp.

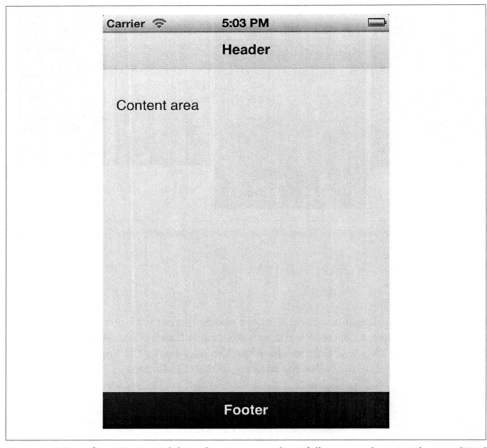

Figure 8-8. One of our jQuery Mobile applications opened as a full-screen webapp in iPhone and iPad

For example, we can have a special jQuery Mobile page inviting the user to install or use our webapp from the home screen menu:

```
if (navigator.standalone!=undefined) {
    // It's iOS
    if (!navigator.standalone) {
        // It's in Safari
        $.mobile.changePage($("#install"), {transition: "none"});
    }
}
```

With the previous code inside mobileinit, then the user will see the install page when our webapp is opened through Safari and she will not be able to use the page. If the user opens the webapp from the home screen menu, then we leave the initial jQuery Mobile page for the user.

Styling the Webapp

Apple provides us some other `meta` tags to style our webapp. First thing we can change is the status bar color (at the top of the screen) using the meta tag `apple-mobile-web-app-status-bar-style` accepting values of `default` (gray), `black`, and `black-translucent`. The latest option will be a transparent black area, so it will take part of our jQuery Mobile's header color. In Figure 8-9 we can see the three values at work:

```
<meta name="apple-mobile-web-app-status-bar-style" content="black">
```

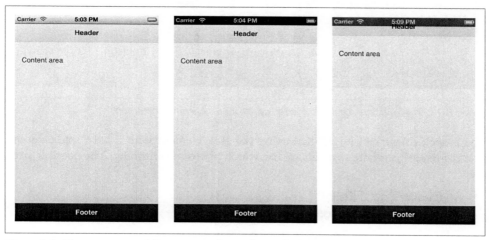

Figure 8-9. Here we can see different status bar styles applied on the same page

 If we are using a `black-translucent` status bar style, we will have available the full height of the browser. That means that the status bar will float over our web page. If we are not using fixed toolbars and we don't leave 20 pixels at the top, it may create a bad experience.

The other change we can make to our chrome-less webapp is to define a launch image. A launch image is used by the operating system as the image that is animated when the app is opening, as shown in Figure 8-10.

Figure 8-10. The launch image is used in the application's opening animation

The launch image can be defined using the `link` element with a `rel="apple-touch-startup-image"`, and the size depends on which platform is running. The possible sizes are:

- All iPhone/iPod: 320×460
- All iPad Portrait: 748×1004
- All iPad Landscape: 748×1024 (rotated 90 degrees)

 Unfortunately, using media queries to add a high definition image for iPhone 4, 4S, and iPod Touch 4th generation is not working. The only work-around is to use some JavaScript to create the `link` element dynamically. In this case, the image should be 640×920.

If we provide only one image, it should be 320×460 (20 pixels are used by the top status bar) and it will work in all iPhones and iPod Touch (including high definitions). It will not work on iPad and the normal launch image will be used (a screenshot taken on the last usage of the webapp):

```
<link rel="apple-touch-startup-image" href="images/launch.png">
```

 If you have an iOS device, you can take a screenshot by pressing the Home button and Power button at the same time. Then, we can use this image as the launch image, so it will coincide with the first load of the webapp.

The different sizes can be defined in different `link` elements with CSS media queries inside the `media` attribute. It doesn't use the `sizes` attribute as in icon definition:

```
<link rel="apple-touch-startup-image" href="images/launch-iphone.png"
    media="(max-device-width: 480px)">
<link rel="apple-touch-startup-image" href="images/launch-iPad-p.png"
    media="screen and (min-device-width: 481px) and (max-device-width: 1024px)
    and (orientation:portrait)">
<link rel="apple-touch-startup-image" href="images/launch-iPad-l.png"
    media="screen and (min-device-width: 481px) and (max-device-width: 1024px)
    and (orientation:landscape)">
```

Mixing It All Together

A jQuery Mobile template for offline access with all the icons and chrome-less webapp
configuration will look like:

```
<!DOCTYPE HTML>
<-- HTML definition with Offline Application Cache manifest -->
<html manifest="offline.appcache">
<head>
 <meta charset="UTF-8">
 <title>short title</title>
 <meta name="viewport" content="width=device-width,user-scalable=no">

 <-- jQuery Mobile files with custom theme -->
 <link rel="stylesheet"
     href="http://code.jquery.com/mobile/1.0/jquery.mobile.structure-1.0.min.css" />
 <link rel="stylesheet" href="custom_theme.css">
 <script src="http://code.jquery.com/jquery-1.6.4.min.js"></script>
 <script src="http://code.jquery.com/jquery-1.6.4.min.js"></script>
 <script src="http://code.jquery.com/mobile/1.0/jquery.mobile-1.0.min.js">
     </script>

 <-- Icons -->
 <link rel="icon" href="icons/icon32.png">
 <link rel="shortcut icon" href="icons/icon32.png">

 <link rel="apple-touch-icon" href="icons/icon57.png" sizes="57x57">
 <link rel="apple-touch-icon" href="icons/icon114.png" sizes="114x114">
 <link rel="apple-touch-icon" href="icons/icon72.png" sizes="72x72">
 <link rel="apple-touch-icon" sizes="80x80" href="icons/icon80.png">
 <link rel="apple-touch-icon-precomposed" sizes="android-only" href="icons/icon57.png">

 <-- If we want to have a chrome-less webapp -->
 <meta name="apple-mobile-web-app-capable" content="yes">
 <meta name="apple-mobile-web-app-status-bar-style" content="black">
 <link rel="apple-touch-startup-image" href="images/launch-iphone.png"
     media="(max-device-width: 480px)">
 <link rel="apple-touch-startup-image" href="images/launch-iPad-p.png"
     media="screen and (min-device-width: 481px) and (max-device-width: 1024px)
     and (orientation:portrait)">
 <link rel="apple-touch-startup-image" href="images/launch-iPad-l.png"
     media="screen and (min-device-width: 481px) and (max-device-width: 1024px)
     and (orientation:landscape)">

</head>
```

```
<body>

<!-- jQuery Mobile's pages -->

</body>
```

Storing Offline Data

To store information locally while we are offline—or even online but we don't want to use AJAX— HTML5-related technologies offer us three options:

- Web Storage API
- Web SQL Database API
- IndexedDB API

 You can check current compatibility of every HTML5-related API on *http://mobilehtml5.org*.

In this book we are going to use the Web Storage API because it's the simplest one and the most compatible API between A-grade jQuery Mobile browsers. This is a very simple API supporting two key-value based collections: localStorage and sessionStorage.

localStorage is a collection of strings stored persistently on the device and session Storage is pretty similar but it is removed from the system when the browser is closed.

 Usually, we can store up to 5 Mb per host on local storage without any problems. However, most browsers store strings in Unicode, so one character will occupy two bytes. This means that it is safe to store 2.5 Mb of text.

The API is available as a global window attribute, called localStorage, with some methods available, such as getItem and setItem to load and save data to/from the collection.

The standard API can only store strings, but that means that we can store:

- Arrays and objects converted to a JSON-style string
- Simple values
- Comma-separated values
- JavaScript code (that we can evaluate later)
- CSS stylesheets (that we can inject later)
- HTML
- Images in base64 (data URI)

Modern mobile browser support the JSON API that allows us to convert objects to JSON strings using `JSON.stringify(object)` and from string to objects using `JSON.parse(string)`. If the API is not available, you can use the free JSON2 library created by Douglas Crockford at *http://github .com/douglascrockford/JSON-js*.

To store a value we use:

```
localStorage.setItem("name", "value");
```

To get a value:

```
var value = localStorage.getItem("name");
```

## CHAPTER 9

A Complete Webapp

In this chapter we are going to create a full application covering many topics that we've seen before in this book. We are going to create a mobile webapp for a conference. The main objectives will be:

- To be the official app for conference's attendees
- Display an updated session list by room
- Provide useful information about the conference

If you are like me, it's possible that you've attended lots of technical conferences in your life. And, as you know, network connections are usually not working properly. That is why our webapp will work offline on compatible devices and we will even be able to convert it to an offline app once we get through the next chapter.

Webapp Structure

The webapp structure will be simple to cover our functionality. It will cover the following:

- Home page
- Sessions
- Where
- Feedback
- About

Sessions will list all the available slots and every session per room per slot available. The session list will be delivered from the server using a JSON-like object that could be created from a server-side language, such as PHP or Java. We will not cover the server-side generation of this JSON or the Content Management System (CMS) to generate the database.

For iPhone, iPod, and iPad we will provide a chromeless application, so we will try to push the user to install our webapp in his system. If the user doesn't want to install the webapp, we will provide an online version.

Our list of files will include the following HTML documents:

- *index.html* (covering the most used pages)
- *feedback.html*
- *feedback.php*

We will have some images in the `images` folder, including:

- *logo.png*
- *sponsors.png*
- *background.png*
- *launch-ios.png* (for iOS launch image)
- *icon114.png* (for iPhone hi-definition icon)
- *icon72.png* (for iPad icon)
- *icon57.png* (for Android and iPhone low-definition icon)

And, of course, we will include all the jQuery Mobile's files including JavaScript, CSS, and images.

The only resource that we will update constantly is *sessions.json*, a JSON-like object file that will be delivered from the server. A server-side script can dynamically generate it. For performance and offline purposes, we will cache this JSON file using the HTML5 Local Storage API.

Offline Manifest

The entire webapp will be contained in an application cache manifest for compatible devices, so our first file to create is the HTML5 cache manifest file.

Our manifest file will look like:

```
CACHE MANIFEST

CACHE:

# jQuery Mobile's files
jquery.js
jquery.mobile.js
jquery.mobile.css
images/ajax-loader.png
images/icons-18-black.png
images/icons-18-white.png
images/icons-36-black.png
images/icons-36-white.png
```

```
# HTML documents
# index.html is always cached implicitly
feedback.html

# Custom script and CSS
index.js
index.css

# Custom images
logo.png
sponsors.png
background.png

# We don't need to cache iOS icons or launch image as the
# platform will cache it by itself

NETWORK:
# We will go to the network only for the JSON file
# and the script that will receive the feedback
# replace mobilexweb.com with your own domain
http://mobilexweb.com/jqmbook/sessions.json
http://mobilexweb.com/jqmbook/feedback.php
```

 Our webapp, once installed, will not be able to access the whole Internet, as we are not supporting * in the NETWORK: section of our offline manifest.

Pages

Let's start with the main *index.html* file. It will be a typical jQuery Mobile document with all the headers that we've covered in this book (including meta tags, icons, and a viewport metatag). It will include all the pages except the form because they are the most probable pages that the user will access every time. We can decide later to move the internal pages to external HTML files. The #sessions page will be the master list, and we will also have a #details page that will be the template for the session detail.

In the #main page, we've decided not to use a header and have replaced it with the conference's main logo. We will use a header on the rest of the pages.

 We will not provide any session information in the HTML document, because we are going to fill them using JavaScript from our JSON-like object retrieved from the server using AJAX. That is why the #sessions and #details pages are without information.

Here is the markup for the *index.html* file:

```
<!DOCTYPE HTML>
<html manifest="manifest.appcache">
<head>
<meta charset="UTF-8">
```

```
<title>jQM Conference</title>
<meta name="viewport" content="width=device-width,user-scalable=no">
<link rel="stylesheet" href="jquery.mobile-1.0.css" />
<link rel="stylesheet" href="index.css" />
<script src="jquery.js"></script>
<script src="index.js"></script>
<script src="jquery.mobile-1.0.js"></script>
<meta name="apple-mobile-web-app-capable" content="yes">
<meta name="apple-mobile-web-app-status-bar-style" content="black">
<link rel="apple-touch-icon" sizes="80x80" href="icons/icon80.png">
<link rel="apple-touch-icon" href="images/icon57.png" sizes="57x57">
<link rel="apple-touch-icon" href="images/icon114.png" sizes="114x114">
<link rel="apple-touch-icon" href="images/icon72.png" sizes="72x72">
<link rel="apple-touch-icon-precomposed" sizes="android-only"
   href="images/icon57.png">
</head>

<body>

<!-- **** HOME PAGE **** -->

<div data-role="page" id="home">

  <div data-role="content">
    <p><img src="images/logo.png" alt="jQM Conference" width="300" height="62"
        align="middle">
        </p>
    <h3>November 5th</h3>
    <div class="ui-grid-a">
      <div class="ui-block-a"><a href="http://www.twitter.com/fakeaccount"
          data-role="button" data-theme="b" target="_blank">Twitter</a></div>
      <div class="ui-block-b"><a href="http://www.facebook.com/fakeaccount"
          data-role="button" data-theme="b" target="_blank">Facebook</a></div>
    </div>
  </div>

  <div data-role="footer" data-position="fixed" data-id="toolbar">
    <div data-role="navbar">
      <ul>
        <li><a class="ui-btn-active" href="#home" data-icon="home"
              data-transition="fade">
              Home</a></li>
        <li><a href="#sessions" data-icon="grid" data-transition="fade">Sessions</a>
        </li>
        <li><a href="#where" data-icon="info" data-transition="fade">Where</a></li>
        <li><a href="#about" data-icon="star" data-transition="fade">About</a></li>
        <li><a href="feedback.html" data-icon="plus" data-rel="dialog">Feedback</a>
        </li>
      </ul>
    </div>
  </div>

</div>

<!-- **** SESSIONS PAGE **** -->
```

```
<div data-role="page" id="sessions">

  <div data-role="header">
    <h1>Sessions</h1>
    <a href='javascript:refresh();' data-icon="refresh" id="refresh" data-theme="c"
        class="ui-btn-left" data-iconpos="notext"></a>
  </div>

  <div data-role="content">
    <p id="console"></p>
    <ul data-role="list-view" data-inset="true" id="slots">
    </ul>
  </div>

  <div data-role="footer" data-position="fixed" data-id="toolbar">
    <div data-role="navbar">
      <ul>
        <li><a href="#home" data-icon="home" data-transition="fade">Home</a></li>
        <li><a class="ui-btn-active" href="#sessions" data-icon="grid"
                data-transition="fade">Sessions</a></li>
        <li><a href="#where" data-icon="info" data-transition="fade">Where</a></li>
        <li><a href="#about" data-icon="star" data-transition="fade">About</a></li>
        <li><a href="feedback.html" data-icon="plus" data-rel="dialog">Feedback</a>
        </li>
      </ul>
    </div>
  </div>

</div>

<!-- **** SESSION'S DETAILS PAGE **** -->

<div data-role="page" id="details" data-add-back-btn="true">

  <div data-role="header">
    <h1>Session detail</h1>
  </div>

  <div data-role="content">
    <div id="sessionInfo"> </div>
  </div>

  <div data-role="footer" data-position="fixed" data-id="toolbar">
   <div data-role="navbar">
    <ul>
     <li><a href="#home" data-icon="home" data-transition="fade">Home</a></li>
     <li><a href="#sessions" data-icon="grid" data-transition="fade">Sessions</a></li>
     <li><a href="#where" data-icon="info" data-transition="fade">Where</a></li>
     <li><a href="#about" data-icon="star" data-transition="fade">About</a></li>
     <li><a href="feedback.html" data-icon="plus" data-rel="dialog">Feedback</a></li>
    </ul>
   </div>
  </div>
```

```
    </div>

    <!-- **** WHERE PAGE **** -->

    <div data-role="page" id="where">

      <div data-role="header">
        <h1>Where</h1>
      </div>

      <div data-role="content">
        Hasta la vista 1234, ACME City

      </div>

      <div data-role="footer" data-position="fixed" data-id="toolbar">
        <div data-role="navbar">
          <ul>
            <li><a href="#home" data-icon="home" data-transition="fade">Home</a></li>
            <li><a href="#sessions" data-icon="grid" data-transition="fade">Sessions</a>
            </li>
            <li><a class="ui-btn-active" href="#where" data-icon="info"
                   data-transition="fade">Where</a></li>
            <li><a href="#about" data-icon="star" data-transition="fade">About</a></li>
            <li><a href="feedback.html" data-icon="plus" data-rel="dialog">Feedback</a>
            </li>
          </ul>
        </div>
      </div>

    </div>

    <!-- **** ABOUT PAGE **** -->

    <div data-role="page" id="about">

      <div data-role="header">
        <h1>About</h1>
      </div>

      <div data-role="content">
        <div data-role="collapsible">
            <h3>Organization</h3>
            <p>This congress is organized by ACME</p>
        </div>
        <div data-role="collapsible">
            <h3>Dates</h3>
            <p>November 5th, 2015 9am to 6pm</p>
        </div>
        <div data-role="collapsible">
            <h3>History</h3>
            <p>First edition of this congress was........</p>
        </div>
        <div data-role="collapsible">
            <h3>Sponsors</h3>
```

```
            <img src="images/sponsors.png" width="300" height="400">
        </div>
    </div>

    <div data-role="footer" data-position="fixed" data-id="toolbar">
        <div data-role="navbar">
            <ul>
                <li><a href="#home" data-icon="home" data-transition="fade">Home</a></li>
                <li><a href="#sessions" data-icon="grid" data-transition="fade">Sessions</a>
                </li>
                <li><a href="#where" data-icon="info" data-transition="fade">Where</a></li>
                <li><a class="ui-btn-active" href="#about" data-icon="star"
                        data-transition="fade">About</a></li>
                <li><a href="feedback.html" data-icon="help" data-transition="fade">Feedback
                </a></li>
            </ul>
        </div>
    </div>

</div>

<!-- **** iOS INSTALLATION DIALOG PAGE **** -->
<div data-role="page" id="ios">

    <div data-role="header">
        <h1>installation</h1>
    </div>

    <div data-role="content">
        <p id="consoleInstall">Complete the installation</p>
        <div id="install">
            <p>To finish the installation, you must add this webapp to your Home Screen.
                To do that, touch the arrow and select "Add to Home Screen"</p>
        </div>
        <a href="javascript:openWithoutInstallation()" class="openWithoutInstall">Open
            without installation</a>
    </div>

</div>

</body>
</html>
```

 We are using a persistent footer, so our navigation bar will not being animated while transitioning between pages.

We can see on the sessions page that we have a blank p element, with ID console and a listview component with the ID slots. We will fill these elements using JavaScript after this page is shown on screen. The same happens for the map element on the where page.

Remember that if we are using a `navbar`, we need to inject it on every page (internal or external) in that page's header or footer. If we don't want to duplicate code, we can inject it using JavaScript on every page. The only optional difference we can have on every page's navbar is the selected element.

The form will be a dialog page in a *feedback.html* external file. Here is the code for that file:

```
<!DOCTYPE HTML>
<html>
<head>
<meta charset="UTF-8">
<title>jQM Conference</title>
<meta name="viewport" content="width=device-width,user-scalable=no">
<link rel="stylesheet" href="jquery.mobile-1.0.css" />
<script src="jquery.js"></script>
<script src="script.js"></script>
<script src="jquery.mobile-1.0.js"></script>
</head>

<body>

<div data-role="dialog">

  <div data-role="header">
    <h1>Feedback</h1>
  </div>

  <div data-role="content">
    <form action="feedback.php" method="post" data-transition="none">

      <div data-role="fieldcontain">
        <label for="name">Name:</label>
        <input type="text" name="name" id="name" value="" required />
      </div>

      <div data-role="fieldcontain">
        <label for="email">Email:</label>
        <input type="email" name="email" id="email" value="" required />
      </div>

      <div data-role="fieldcontain">
        <label for="comments">Comments:</label>
        <textarea cols="40" rows="8" name="comments" id="comments"></textarea>
      </div>

         <div data-role="fieldcontain">
        <label for="contacted">Can we contact you?</label>
        <select name="contacted" id="contacted" data-role="slider">
          <option value="no">No</option>
          <option value="yes">Yes</option>
        </select>
      </div>
```

```
            <input type="submit" value="Send" data-theme="a">

        </form>
    </div>

</div>
</body>
</html>
```

 We are not covering validation on the client- and server-side. Remember always to validate a form's data before processing it.

The *feedback.php* file should validate the information, store it on a database or send it by email, and show a jQuery Mobile page as a result:

```
<!DOCTYPE HTML>
<html>
<head>
<meta charset="UTF-8">
<title>jQM Conference</title>
<meta name="viewport" content="width=device-width,user-scalable=no">
<link rel="stylesheet" href="jquery.mobile-1.0.css" />
<script src="jquery.js"></script>
<script src="script.js"></script>
<script src="jquery.mobile-1.0.js"></script>
</head>

<body>

<div data-role="dialog">

  <div data-role="header">
    <h1>Feedback</h1>
  </div>

  <div data-role="content">

      <?php
          // Validation and processing here

          ?>
      Thanks for your feedback.

      <a data-role="button" data-inverse="true" href="index.html">Close</a>

  </div>

</div>
</body>
</html>
```

Stylesheet

We have some custom styles defined in *index.css*:

```css
/* Some styles for header */
.ui-header {
        background-color: #69C;
        background-image: url('images/background.png');
        background-position: top right;
        background-repeat: no-repeat
}

/* Some styles for offline installation process */
#console, #consoleInstall {
        background-color: #FF6;
        border-radius: 10px;
        -webkit-border-radius: 10px;
        padding: 5px;
        margin: 0;
        text-align: center;
        border: 1px solid #CCC;
        font-size: small;
}

/* Home's content area */
#home [data-role=content] {
        background-color: white;
        text-align: center;
}

/* Buttons */
.openWithoutInstall {
        margin-top: 50px;
        display: block;
}

/* Navbar text */
[data-role=navbar] .ui-btn-text {
      font-size: smaller;
}
```

Data

The JSON file with the information about sessions will have a structure like in the following sample:

```json
{
  "slots":
   [
     // Some slots are special times -opening, breaks, lunch, etc.-
     { "id": 1, "time": "09:00", "message": "Opening" },
     // Some slots are session times
     { "id": 2, "time": "09:20"}
   ],
  "sessions":
```

```
[
    { "id": 1, "title": "A great session", "timeId": 2,
      "description": "...", "speaker": "...", "room": "..." }
]
}
```

Script

We have several functionalities that will work only with JavaScript, including:

- iOS chromeless detection
- Session data download
- Session list and session details dynamic page generation

Here is the code for the *index.js* file:

```
var data;

$(document).bind("mobileinit", function() {

        if (navigator.platform=="iPhone" || navigator.platform=="iPad" ||
                navigator.platform=="iPod" || navigator.platform=="iPad" ||
                navigator.platform=="iPhone Simulator" ) {

                // It's an iOS device, we check if we are in chrome-less mode
                if (!navigator.standalone) {
                        showIOSInvitation();
                }
        }

        /* We capture the sessions page load to check dynamic session data */
        $("#sessions").live("pageshow", function() {

                if (window.localStorage!=undefined) {
                        // HTML5 Local Storage is available
                        if (window.localStorage.getItem("data")!=undefined &&
                                        window.localStorage.getItem("data")!=null) {
                                // We first load the offline stored session
                                // information while checking updates
                                showSessions(window.localStorage.getItem("data"));
                                $("#console").html("Checking data update");
                        } else {
                                // There is no local storage cache
                                $("#console").html("Downloading session data...");
                        }
                } else {
                        // No HTML5 Local Storage, downloading JSON every time
                        $("#console").html("Downloading session data...");
                }

                loadSessionsAjax();
        });

});
```

```
function showIOSInvitation() {
  setTimeout(function() {
        // We hide the saving information until the whole webapp is downloaded
        $("#install").hide();
        // We open the iOS instructions for adding to the homepage
        $.mobile.changePage($("#ios"), {transition: "slideup",
            changeHash: false});
  }, 100);

  // We capture HTML5 Application Cache events to provide useful information
  if (window.applicationCache!=undefined) {
        window.applicationCache.addEventListener('checking', function() {
                $("#consoleInstall").html("Checking version");
        });

        window.applicationCache.addEventListener('downloading', function() {
                $("#consoleInstall").html("Downloading application.
                    Please wait...");
        });

        window.applicationCache.addEventListener('cached', function() {
                $("#consoleInstall").html("Application downloaded");
                $("#install").show();
        });

        window.applicationCache.addEventListener('updateready', function() {
                $("#consoleInstall").html("Application downloaded");
                $("#install").show();
        });
        window.applicationCache.addEventListener('noupdate', function() {
                $("#consoleInstall").html("Application downloaded");
                $("#install").show();
        });
        window.applicationCache.addEventListener('error', function(e) {
                $("#consoleInstall").html("There was an error downloading this
                    app");
        });
        window.applicationCache.addEventListener('obsolete', function(e) {
                $("#consoleInstall").html("There was an error downloading this
                    app");
        });
        }

}

function loadSessionsAjax() {
  // We bring the JSON as text so it's easy to store in Local Storage
    $.ajax(/*"http://www.mobilexweb.com/congress/*/"sessions.json", {
      complete: function(xhr) {
          if (window.localStorage!=undefined) {
                if (window.localStorage.getItem("data")!=undefined &&
                    window.localStorage.getItem("data")!=null) {
                    if (xhr.responseText==window.localStorage.getItem("data")) {
                        // The new session downloaded is the same as the
```

```
                                    // one in screen
                                    $("#console").html("Schedule is updated");
                        } else {
                                    // There is an update on the session data
                                    if (confirm("There is an update in the schedule
                                        available, do you want to load it now?")) {
                                            $("#console").html("Schedule is updated");
                                            showSessions(xhr.responseText);
                                    } else {
                                            $("#console").html("Schedule will be
                                                updated later");
                                    }
                        }
                } else {
                            // Local Storage is available but no previous
                            // cache found
                            $("#console").html("Schedule is updated");
                            showSessions(xhr.responseText);
                }
        } else {
                    // No Local Storage, show the info without saving
                    $("#console").html("Schedule is updated");
                    showSessions(xhr.responseText);
        }
    },
    dataType: 'text',
    error: function() {
            $("#console").html("Schedule update could not be downloaded");
    }
});
}


var isFirstLoad = true;

function showSessions(string) {
        if (window.JSON!=undefined) {
                data = JSON.parse(string);
        } else {
            data = eval("(" + string + ")");
        }
        if (window.localStorage!=undefined) {
                // Save the new data as string
                window.localStorage.setItem("data", string);
        }

        $("#slots").html("");

        var html = "";
        for (var i=0; i<data.slots.length; i++) {

                if (data.slots[i].message!=null) {
                    // This is an special slot, so we create a divider
                    html += "<li data-role='list-divider' data-groupingtheme='e'>" +
                        data.slots[i].time + ": " + data.slots[i].message  + "</li>";
```

```
                } else {
                        // This is a normal slot with sessions
                        html += "<li><a href='javascript:showDetails(" + i + ")'
                            >Sessions of " +
                            data.slots[i].time + "</a></li>";
                }
        }

        $("#slots").html(html);

        if (isFirstLoad) {
                $("#slots").listview();
                isFirstLoad = false;
        } else {
                $("#slots").listview('refresh');
        }

}

function showDetails(index) {
        $("#details h1").html("Sessions of " + data.slots[index].time);
        var html = ""
        for (var i=0; i<data.sessions.length; i++) {
                if (data.sessions[i].timeId==data.slots[index].id) {
                        // We create one collapsible component per session
                        html += "<div data-role='collapsible'>";
                        html += "<h3>" + data.sessions[i].title + "</h3>";
                        html +=" <h3>" + data.sessions[i].room + "</h3>";
                        html += "<h4>Speaker/s: " + data.sessions[i].speaker;
                        html += "</h4>";
                        html += "<p>" + data.sessions[i].description + "</p>";
                        html += "</div>";
                }
        }
        // We provide the information to the details page
        $("#sessionInfo").html(html);
        $("#sessionInfo div").collapsible();

        // We change to the details page
        $.mobile.changePage($("#details"));
}

function refresh() {
        $("#console").html("Verifying...");
        loadSessionsAjax();
}

function openWithoutInstallation() {
        // We remove the dialog-like iOS installation page
        $.mobile.changePage($("#home"), {transition:"slideup", reverse:true});
}
```

For Android and other platforms, we can create hybrids or widgets and provide a similar installation page linking to the native package from our servers or from a store.

There is plenty of room here for improvement. For example, we can create a URL for each session such as #details!22 so we can track this URL and provide deep linking dynamic detail loading. Figure 9-1 shows our webapp working as a browser-based app and as an offline chromeless application on iOS devices.

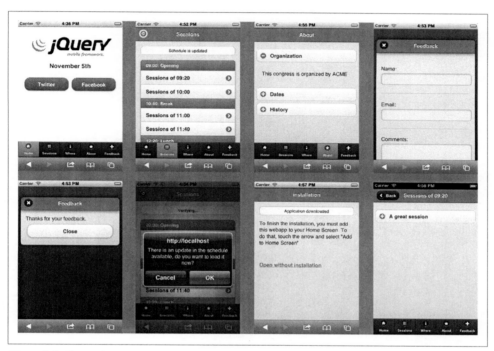

Figure 9-1. Our webapp

## CHAPTER 10

Extending the Framework

jQuery is well-known for its great plug-in community. jQuery Mobile is also a platform that can be extended easily though third-party plug-ins. An updated list of jQuery Mobile plug-ins to use can be found in *http://mobilexweb.com/go/jqmplugin*.

jQuery can be extended in many ways. We can create:

Themes
> A CSS file and/or a couple of images

Plug-ins
> A JavaScript and a CSS file that provides new widgets (`data-role`) to the framework

Extensions
> A JavaScript file that adds new behavior to current jQuery Mobile widgets and/or core functionality

Creating a Plug-in

jQuery Mobile architecture is based on jQuery UI framework, so creating plug-ins for the mobile framework is similar to the UI framework.

First, we need to understand a few things to create compatible plug-ins:

- We should honor the compatibility from jQuery Mobile. Creating a plug-in that is only compatible with one or two platforms will not be useful for the community.
- To use the plug-in, the user should just add a script file and a CSS file.
- We should use `data-*` attributes as much as possible to continue the framework architecture.
- The plug-in should work properly with custom namespacing and the theming framework.
- The plug-in should auto-initialize widgets as in the main framework.
- Use semantic HTML5 as much as possible to define your plug-in's contents.

- Use accessibility features (ARIA for example) if applicable.
- To avoid future framework incompatibilities, avoid using generic names for your own custom `data-role` values. For example, avoid using `tableview` or `datepicker`, because future versions of the framework could include some of this behavior.

 HTML5, CSS3, ARIA, and other features are outside the scope of this book. To create a good and compatible widget, you should be confident with all these technologies.

Basic Template

A widget should be initialized in two ways:

- Auto initialization, meaning automatic creation through data roles or semantic HTML5 code
- Explicit initialization through the widget name using jQuery syntax, for example: `$("#myelement").widgetname()`

The first step in creating a widget is to select a name. Try to choose a name that will not conflict with future widgets.

The widget should use one JavaScript file named *jquery.mobile.<plugin-name>.js* and an optional +*jquery.mobile.<plugin-name>.css* file.

The widget template is:

```
(function($){
    // We wrap all the code inside this function to be sure that $ is
    // linked to the jQuery global object

    // Widget definition
    $.widget("mobile.ourWidgetName", $.mobile.widget, {
        options: {
        // Here we can create default options of our widget
        },
        // Private methods
        _create: function() {
            // The constructor function
        },


        // Public methods

        enable: function() {
            // Enable the widget
        },
        disable: function() {
            // Disable the widget
        },
        refresh: function() {
            // Refresh the widget
```

```
        }
    });
    // End of widget definition

    // Auto-initialization code
    $(document).bind("pagecreate", function(event) {
        // We find data-role's and apply our widget constructor
        $(event.target).find(":jqmData(role='ourWidgetName')").ourWidgetName();

    });

}(jQuery));
```

Creating Our Plug-in

As a sample, we are going to create a dynamic image widget that will use the free service Sencha IO Src. This cloud-based service takes an image source and resizes it on the server based on the current mobile browser dimensions.

 You can find the official documentation of the Sencha IO Src service at *http://mobilexweb.com/go/senchaio.*

We will call our widget `dynamicimage`. We can take any `img` element and apply our widget automatically or we can use a new `data-role` called `dynamic-image`. We will choose the latter option in the following pages.

Usage

The idea is that we can define an `img` with a `data-src` attribute that will load a Sencha IO Src image. We decide to not use the standard `src` attribute because it will cause a double load, the original file and the resized file.

We will have two special attributes, `data-width` will define the percentage of the device's screen and `data-margin` will define a margin that will be deducted from current device's screen.

We won't apply theming because images don't have any jQuery Mobile visualization.

The widget

Every widget is defined as an object with properties and functions. A function starting with underscore will be a private function. Inside a function, `this` will refer to the widget object and `this.element` will refer to the HTML element:

```
$.widget("mobile.dynamicimage", $.mobile.widget, {
    options: {
        width: "100%",
        margin: 0
```

```
        }
    });
```

The constructor is always called _create. It is called once, when the widget is initialized for the first time. We can use this.options to access the options collection.

Our create function will be like this:

```
$.widget("mobile.dynamicimage", $.mobile.widget, {
    options: {
        width: 100,
        margin: 0
    },
    _create: function() {
        // We call a private function
        this._loadURL();
    }
});
```

Every public function (not starting with underscore) can be called using the widget syntax and usually we need to support at least refresh, enable, and disable functions, as they are common inside jQuery Mobile. For example, if we change a URL of an image using JavaScript, we can call a refresh action on our widget using $("#ourImage").dynam icimage("refresh"). It will call the public refresh function.

We will define the refresh, enable, and disable functions:

```
$.widget("mobile.dynamicimage", $.mobile.widget, {
    options: {
        width: 100,
        margin: 0
    },
    _create: function() {
        // We call a private function
        this._loadURL();
    },
    // Public methods
    enable: function() {
        // Enable the widget
        $(this.element).attr('disabled', '');
    },
    disable: function() {
        // Disable the widget
        $(this.element).removeAttr('disabled');
    },
    refresh: function() {
        // Refresh the widget
        this._loadURL();
    }
});
```

Finally, our core method, the _loadURL private function:

```
_loadURL: function() {
        // this.element will be our +img+ element
```

```
var url; // we create the service URL
url = "http://src.sencha.io/";

var parameters = "";
if (!isNaN(this.options.width)) {
        parameters += "x" + this.options.width;
}
if ((!isNaN(this.options.margin)) && this.options.margin>0) {
        parameters += "-" + this.options.margin;
}
if (parameters.length>0) {
        url += parameters + "/";
}

// Sencha IO needs an absolute URL
var originalUrl = $(this.element).jqmData("src");
if (originalUrl.length>1) {
        var newUrl = "";
        if ($.mobile.path.isAbsoluteUrl(originalUrl)) {
                // The image URL is already absolute
                newUrl = originalUrl;
        } else {
                // The image URL is relative, we create an absolute one
                var baseUrl = $.mobile.path.parseUrl(location.href);
                var baseUrlWithoutScript = baseUrl.protocol + "//" +
                        baseUrl.host + baseUrl.directory;
                newUrl = $.mobile.path.makeUrlAbsolute(originalUrl,
                        baseUrlWithoutScript);
        }

        url += newUrl;

        $(this.element).attr("src", url);
}
```

Auto-initialization

With this widget code, we can add the auto-initialization code that will look for every
data-role="dynamic-image" element and will create our widget:

```
$(document).bind("pagecreate", function(event) {
    // We find data-role's and apply our widget constructor
    $(event.target).find("img:jqmData(role='dynamic-image')").dynamicimage();
});
```

> If we use jqmData instead of attr, we are custom namespace compatible.
> Every data-* attribute on our element will be mapped automatically to
> this.options inside our widget object.

Using our plug-in

First, we need to add the JavaScript file after the jQuery Mobile JavaScript include:

```
<script src="jquery.mobile-dynamicimage-1.0.js"></script>
```

And then we just need to create `img` elements with the right parameters:

```
<-- Image taking the device's 100% width -->
<img data-src="images/photo.png" data-role="dynamic-image">

<-- Image taking the device's 40% width -->
<img data-src="images/photo.png" data-role="dynamic-image" data-width="40">

<-- Image taking the device's 100% width with 20 pixels of margin -->
<img data-src="images/photo.png" data-role="dynamic-image" data-margin="50">
```

Our plug-in can be seen in Figure 10-1.

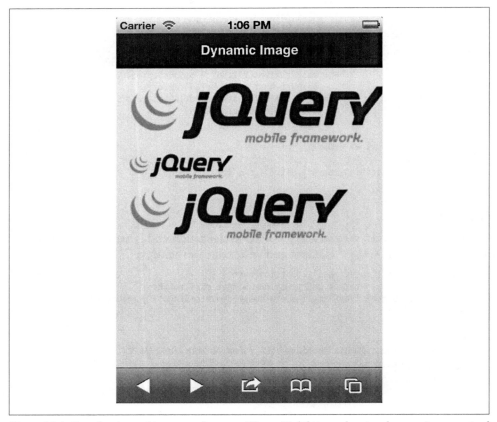

Figure 10-1. Our plug-in working properly on our jQuery Mobile page showing the same image resized on the Sencha IO Src service

Full source code

Following is the full source code for *jquery.mobile-dynamicimage-1.0.js*:

```javascript
(function($){
    // Widget definition
    $.widget( "mobile.dynamicimage", $.mobile.widget, {
        options: {
            margin: 0, width: 100
        },
        _create: function() {
            this._loadURL();
        },

            // Private methods
            _loadURL: function() {
                // this.element will be our +img+ element

                var url; // we create the service URL
                url = "http://src.sencha.io/";

                var parameters = "";
                if (!isNaN(this.options.width)) {
                    parameters += "x" + this.options.width;
                }
                if ((!isNaN(this.options.margin)) && this.options.margin>0) {
                    parameters += "-" + this.options.margin;
                }
                if (parameters.length>0) {
                    url += parameters + "/";
                }

                // Sencha IO needs an absolute URL
                var originalUrl = $(this.element).jqmData("src");
                if (originalUrl.length>1) {
                    var newUrl = "";
                    if ($.mobile.path.isAbsoluteUrl(originalUrl)) {
                        // The image URL is already absolute
                        newUrl = originalUrl;
                    } else {
                        // The image URL is relative, we create an
                        // absolute one
                        var baseUrl = $.mobile.path.parseUrl(location.href);
                        var baseUrlWithoutScript = baseUrl.protocol + "//"
                            + baseUrl.host + baseUrl.directory;
                        newUrl = $.mobile.path.makeUrlAbsolute(originalUrl,
                            baseUrlWithoutScript);
                    }

                    url += newUrl;

                    $(this.element).attr("src", url);
                }
            },

            // Public methods
```

```
                    enable: function() {
                        // Enable the widget
                                $(this.element).attr('disabled', '');
                    },
                    disable: function() {
                        // Disable the widget
                                $(this.element).removeAttr('disabled');
                    },
                    refresh: function() {
                        // Refresh the widget
                                this._loadURL();
                    }
            });
            // End of widget definition

            // Auto-initialization code
            $(document).bind("pagecreate", function(event) {
                // We find data-role's and apply our widget constructor
                $(event.target).find("img:jqmData(role='dynamic-image')").dynamicimage();

            });

    }(jQuery));
```

Notable Plug-ins

There are some great plug-ins out there. The following list describes the most useful plug-ins that we can use today in our jQuery Mobile projects.

Pagination

The pagination plug-in (shown in Figure 10-2) can be found on *http://filamentgroup .com/lab/jquery_mobile_pagination_plugin* and allows jQuery Mobile to paginate content, such as images. It provides a right arrow and left arrow on the screen so the user understands he can move forward and backward.

The user can move between pages with:

- Taps on the arrow buttons floating on the screen
- Using left and right arrow keys on devices with keyboards
- Swiping left and right using drag touch events

When we download the framework we will find two files

- *jquery.mobile.pagination.css*
- *jquery.mobile.pagination.js*

After including these two files on our head element, we need to create a ul element with data-role="pagination". Every jQuery Mobile page should have a pagination widget inside.

Figure 10-2. Pagination plug-in in action showing a couple of images as different pages

Every pagination widget will have two li elements with a links inside to the previous and next pages. The li elements will have two classes: ui-pagination-prev for the previous page and ui-pagination-next for the next page. For example:

```
<ul data-role="pagination">
    <li class="ui-pagination-prev"><a href="1.html">Prev</a></li>
    <li class="ui-pagination-next"><a href="3.html">Next</a></li>
</ul>
```

Bartender

This plug-in is available for free at *http://www.stokkers.mobi/valuables/bartender.html*
provides a bottom tab bar navigation inspired in native iOS applications as we can see
in Figure 10-3.

This plug-in is just a CSS file and a couple of images, so there are no `data-*` elements
to use; just some class definitions.

The usual template code will be implemented on a fixed footer in a normal `navbar`
widget and it will look like:

```
<div data-role="navbar" data-grid="d">
   <ul class="apple-navbar-ui comboSprite">
      <-- elements -->
   </ul>
</div>
```

The plug-in also supports tabs with count bubbles, as in iOS using `<span class="ui-li-count">XXXX</span>` inside an `li` element.

DateBox

DateBox provides a date-picker selector (as shown in Figure 10-4) using jQuery Mobile
syntax. It is defined by a `data-role="datebox"` that can be applied to any `<input
type="date">` element. It is fully customizable with many options, but the standard code
will look like this:

```
<input type="date" data-role="datebox">
```

The official website for download, samples, and documentation is *http://dev.jtsage.com/
jQM-DateBox* and it provides different modes always as a pop-up layer (Figure 10-5),
including:

- Full calendar selector
- Android mode, a calendar with numeric steppers for date, month, and year
- Slider mode, providing three horizontal sliders: for the year, month, and day
- Flip mode, providing three vertical sliders: for the year, month, and day
- Time mode
- Duration mode

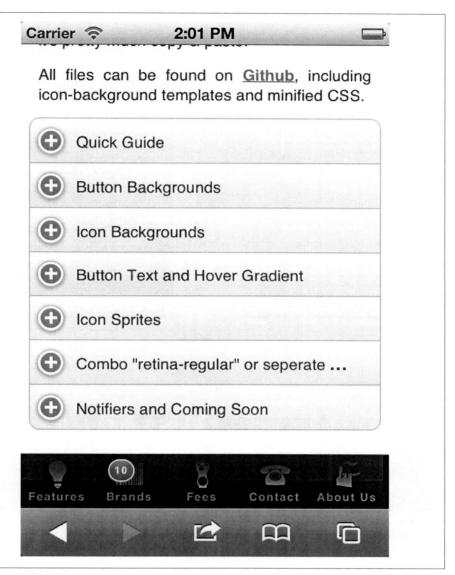

Figure 10-3. Bartender provides an iOS-like tab bar navigation design

Figure 10-4. With DateBox we can create nice date picker selectors, even on devices without HTML5 date input types

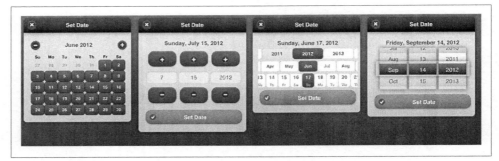

Figure 10-5. DateBox provides different calendar modes for selection

Simple Dialog

With this free plug-in, we can replace the standard `window.alert`, `window.confirm`, and `window.prompt` with a jQuery Mobile style window asking the user for an input as in Figure 10-6.

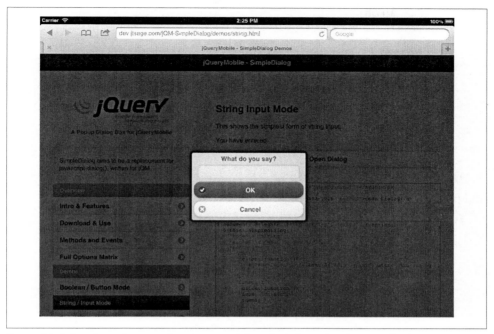

Figure 10-6. Simple Dialog provides jQuery Mobile-style dialogs to replace standard JavaScript pop-up windows

The documentation and download site is *http://dev.jtsage.com/jQM-SimpleDialog*.

To use Simple Dialog, we have to download and add to our head the script file of the plug-in, or use the CDN for the plug-in:

```
<script src="http://dev.jtsage.com/cdn/simpledialog/latest/
    jquery.mobile.simpledialog.min.js"></script>
```

Then when we want to create an alert, we just use the following code snippet:

```
$("#button").click(function() {
    $(this).simpledialog({
        mode: 'bool',  // For normal alert or confirm
        prompt: "We could not open the file",
        useModal: true,
        buttons: [
            'Ok': {
                theme: "c", icon: "check"
            }
        ]
    });
});
```

For a confirmation dialog, the code should look like this:

```
$("#button").click(function() {
    $(this).simpledialog({
```

```
            mode: 'bool',
            prompt: "Do you want to delete this file?",
            useModal: true,
            buttons: [
                'Yes': {
                    theme: "c", icon: "delete",
                    click: function() { // Delete }
                },
                'No': {
                    theme: "a", icon: "cancel"
                },
            ]
        });
    });
```

And finally for a text prompt dialog:

```
$("#button").click(function() {
    $(this).simpledialog({
        mode: 'string',
        prompt: "What is your name?",
        useModal: true,
        buttons: [
            'No': {
                theme: "c", icon: "delete",
                click: function() {
                    alert("Your name is " + $("#button").jqmData("string"));
                }
            }
        ]
    });
});
```

Action Sheet

This is another plug-in inspired by iOS native controls. An Action Sheet is a modal pop-up menu.

We can find the plug-in, both a CSS and JavaScript file at *https://github.com/hiroprota gonist/jquery.mobile.actionsheet*.

To create an Action Sheet we need a button to open it that will be an a element with data-role="actionsheet". When clicked, it will open the next sibling element or the element with the id defined by the data-sheet attribute.

> To use this plug-in, remember to add *jquery.mobile.actionsheet.js* and *jquery.mobile.actionsheet.css* to your head.

This element should have jQuery Mobile's buttons inside. If the user clicks outside the sheet, it will be closed. We can also provide a button with data-rel="close" that will act as the closing/cancel action. For example:

```
<a data-role="actionsheet" data-sheet="share" data-icon="plus">Share</a>

<div id="share">
    <a href="facebook.html" data-role="button">Share in Facebook</a>
    <a href="twitter.html" data-role="button">Share in Twitter</a>
    <a href="google.html" data-role="button">Share in Google+</a>
    <a data-rel="close" data-role="button">Cancel</a>
</div>
```

Plug-ins for Tablets

When we are delivering webapps for tablets, sometimes it's useful to split the page in two columns instead of using a full-width menu as in standard jQuery Mobile. That is why two plug-ins provides us with solutions for tablet applications: SplitView and MultiView.

SplitView

SplitView is available at *http://asyraf9.github.com/jquery-mobile* and it allow us to define two main areas inside a document called panels.

Each panel is a jQuery Mobile page, with a header, content, and footer. A SplitView allows two panels to be on screen at the same time in portrait orientation as seen in Figure 10-7. That means that we will have two pages, typically a menu at the left and a content area at the right.

In portrait orientation, the menu panel is hidden inside a top-left button and it will open as a pop-up menu as seen in Figure 10-8.

Every panel has a data-id attribute defining the name of the panel. This will be useful for links:

```
<body>
  <div data-role="panel" data-id="menu">
    <div data-role="page">

    </div>
  </div>
  <div data-role="panel" data-id="main">
    <div data-role="page">

    </div>
  </div>
</body>
```

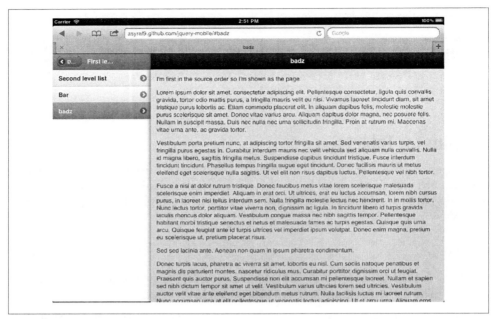

Figure 10-7. With SplitView, we can create tablet applications with support for multiple pages at the same time, typically a menu and a content area

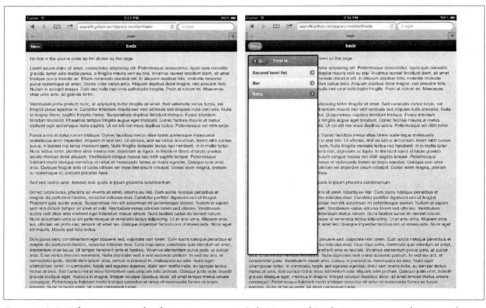

Figure 10-8. When rotating the device to portrait, SplitView and MultiView convert the two columns in one main section with a pop-up menu at the top left corner

After this definition, we can define in every a element the panel in which the link should load. The transition animation will work inside every panel as if they were frames.

For example:

```
<a href="demo.html" data-panel="main">Demos</a>
```

MultiView

MultiView is similar in purpose to SplitView but with a different implementation (Figure 10-9). It also implements a `data-role="panel"` but as children of the `page`.

The plug-in is available as a working demo at *http://www.stokkers.mobi/valuables/multiview/page1.html* and changes the normal behavior of jQuery Mobile. A `data-role="page"` instead of content areas, contains up to four panel (`data-role="panel"`) areas:

- Menu panel
- Main panel
- Full-width panel (optional, for landscape)
- Popover panel (optional, for landscape)

The panel type is defined by `data-id`, for example: `data-id="menu"`.

Every panel contains its own pages, so we will have pages nested inside other pages. The structure will be page → panel → page → header/content/footer. Every panel can have as many pages as necessary, but at least one needs to have `data-show="first"` attribute.

Using `data-target`, we can define on a link where to open that page. It can be:

- Full page load (removing all the panels)
- Panel load (menu or main)
- Multiple load (one page on the menu and one page on the main)

The plug-in doesn't have too much documentation but following the online demo should not be a problem.

Compatible Plug-ins

There are some jQuery (not-mobile) plug-ins that can also be used with jQuery Mobile but they don't follow the rules of the framework. Therefore, no `data-role` or functionality provided using pure JavaScript code.

The following list includes some of these compatible plug-ins:

- Photoswipe (*http://photoswipe.com*): Photo Gallery creator for iOS, Android, and BlackBerry 6+.

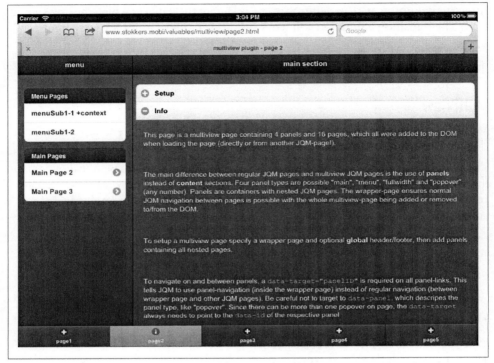

Figure 10-9. With MultiView we can also create tablet-like applications sharing fixed footers between panels

- Diapo (*http://www.pixedelic.com/plugins/diapo*): Slideshow gallery with great CSS animations
- jQuery UI Maps (*http://code.google.com/p/jquery-ui-map*): Provides Google Maps integration inside our mobile webapp
- MobiScroll (*http://www.mobiscroll.com*): Time and date pickers as numeric steppers or wheels

## CHAPTER 11

Packaging for Stores

Some people claim "Stores are the future of apps." To be honest, nobody knows if the future of app distribution will be store-based, browser-based, or a hybrid mechanism. The great thing about using HTML5 content—and jQuery Mobile in particular—is that we can also package our webapp as a native app for store distribution.

Therefore, if you want to distribute your app in application stores, you can definitely do that using jQuery Mobile. There are different approaches for doing that regarding the platform you want to target.

The first thing to understand is that we need to create one package per platform. In some way, we need to copy our files (HTML, JavaScript, CSS, and jQuery Mobile files) in different projects and create different packages.

 There is a group inside W3C working on a future standard for packaging webapps for distribution. The group is Native Web apps and its URL is *http://www.w3.org/community/native-web-apps/*.

When we package a webapp as a native application, we usually have the ability to access some new APIs that are not typically in HTML5, such as Camera, Contacts, or Accelerometer.

To package our webapp for store distribution we can:

- Create a native project for every platform, add our webapp files as local resources, and use a Web View component and bind it to our HTML content. Sometimes this idea is called a hybrid app.
- Use an official webapp platform, which usually means packaging our files in a ZIP archive.
- Use a native compilation framework that helps us to compile our app to multiple platforms.

Compiling our webapp as a native package usually means that we need some expertise in dealing with native code and SDK tools per platform.

Store Distribution

The first step to package our application is to decide which platforms we are going to target and in which stores we are going to distribute our app.

Table 11-1 shows the stores available for distribution. We should create a publisher account on each one.

Table 11-1. Application stores available for distribution

Store	Owner	Platforms	Formats	Publisher cost	URL
AppStore	Apple	iOS (iPhone, iPod, iPad)	ipa	$99 per year	http://developer.apple.com/programs/ios
Android Market	Google	Android	apk	$20 once	http://market.android.com/publish
AppWorld	RIM BlackBerry	Smartphones/PlayBook	cod/bar	Free	http://appworld.blackberry.com/isvportal
Nokia Store	Nokia	Symbian/N9	wgz/deb bar	1 euro	http://info.publish.nokia.com/
Amazon AppStore	Amazon	Android/Kindle Fire	apk	$99 per year	http://developer.amazon.com/
Marketplace	Microsoft	Windows Phone		$99 per year	http://create.msdn.com/

For each platform we will also need to gather some metadata information that we should verify with every store documentation, including:

- Icon in high resolution (usually 512×512)
- Description text
- Category selection
- Screenshots per platform
- Distribution—device list compatibility
- Distribution—country and language
- Marketing banners

Custom Distribution

On some platforms we can also distribute our app through our own web server with the right MIME type configuration. Symbian and BlackBerry devices will receive and install any webapp executable file without problems.

Android and Nokia N9 will install apps from our server if the user allows third-party server installation in her settings.

Other platforms, such as iOS or Windows Phone will never allow the installation from a source other than the official store.

 There are some ways to configure our developer devices to install our own apps but this is only for testing. These techniques are out of the scope of this book.

Preparing the Package

We have to keep in mind some important things when we are creating native-like apps with jQuery Mobile. First, there will be no browser toolbars. That means, for example, no back button from the UI. Our webapp should have back buttons explicitly on the header as we've already seen before in this book.

 When compiling a native app, never use CDN as the way to load jQuery Mobile files.

The second problem will be with loading external pages. When creating an app, we can load local pages that are HTML files that will be distributed with the app itself.

If we want to load jQuery Mobile documents from a remote URL, we can define `$.support.cors=true` on the `mobileinit` event handler. This will allow the framework access via AJAX remote servers. We should also declare `$.mobile.allowCrossDomainPages=true`.

jQuery Mobile also recommends that you disable `pushState` to avoid problems with URL management.

Therefore, our main HTML file should have:

```
$(document).bind("mobileinit", function() {
    $.support.cors = true;
    $.mobile.allowCrossDomainPages = true;
    $.mobile.pushState = false;
});
```

If we are targeting iOS 5.0+, we can also enable the real fixed toolbars functionality for better performance and usability on fixed headers and footers.

 When packaging native apps, we should prepare some other files, such as an icon for the home or app menu and a launch image that will be shown while our webapp is loaded. Some platforms also need an explicit list of servers to access the network.

Packaging with PhoneGap

PhoneGap is an open source platform for compiling native apps from HTML5 code, and it's fully compatible with jQuery Mobile. PhoneGap (also called Apache CallBack) is managed mainly by Adobe and other important companies. Covering PhoneGap fully is out of the scope of this book. The idea here is to give you the basic information to start with it.

With PhoneGap (*http://phonegap.com*) we can compile our jQuery Mobile apps for:

- iOS
- Android
- webOS
- Symbian
- BlackBerry
- Windows Phone

When we download PhoneGap, we will receive a ZIP file with package samples for use with every platform SDK and a JavaScript file to include in every HTML file. Up to PhoneGap 1.2, every platform needs its own JavaScript file. This file will normalize some behaviors between platforms and will add some API compatibility.

 If you want to compile an iOS application, you will need a Mac or a cloud-based service. You can easily rent a Mac device using *http://mac incloud.com*.

On iOS, PhoneGap provides an installation mechanism that adds a PhoneGap project type inside Xcode, the official IDE to create native iOS applications. Table 11-2 shows every SDK you need to have installed for compilation.

Table 11-2. SDKs and IDEs required for native compilation

SDK	Device platform	Desktop platforms	Download URL
Xcode	iOS	Mac OS	Available on Mac AppStore
ADT for Eclipse	Android	Win/Mac/Linux	*http://developer.android.com*
WebWorks SDK	BlackBerry	Win/Mac	*http:// blackberry.com/developers*
Visual Studio for WP	Windows Phone	Win	*http://microsoft.com/visualstudio*
Nokia Web Tools for Symbian	Symbian	Win/Mac	*http://developer.nokia.com*

When we create a project for every platform, we need to copy our files (HTML, Java-Script, CSS, images, etc.) to the right folder on every PhoneGap sample project. Usually it is a folder called *www*. We will find an *index.html* file that we should replace with our own jQuery Mobile webapp files.

PhoneGap Build

If we don't want to get into the mess of creating one package per platform using SDKs, Adobe offers a service—with free and paid plans—to compile apps in the cloud, called PhoneGap Build, available at *http://build.phonegap.com*.

With this service we can upload a ZIP file with our full jQuery Mobile application (including CSS, JavaScript, and images) with a *config.xml* following W3C widget standard, and PhoneGap Build will compile the right package for:

- iOS
- Android
- webOS
- BlackBerry smartphones
- Symbian

At the time of this writing, PhoneGap Build doesn't support Windows Phone or Black-Berry tablet, but it should be available soon.

 For iOS and BlackBerry, we need to provide PhoneGap Build with our own signing keys provided by both platforms' publisher programs.

Index

We'd like to hear your suggestions for improving our indexes. Send email to *index@oreilly.com*.

split button lists, 104–107

C

cache manifest, 184
cached event, 189
caching pages, 48
CDNs (Content Delivery Networks)
    about, 27–29
    latest builds, 29
Champeon, Steven, 17
changeHash property, 153
changePage method, 150, 153
checkboxes, 137
checkboxradio widget, 143
checked attribute, 126
checking event, 189
code syntax assistant (Dreamweaver), 32
collapsible role
    about, 35, 77–78
    nesting, 78
collapsible sets, 35, 79–80
collapsible widget, 143, 151
collapsible-set role, 35, 79–80
color swatches
    about, 36
    customizing for search bar, 113
    defining for buttons, 41, 67
    defining for count bubbles, 112
    defining for lists, 95
    defining for logos, 68
    defining for sliders, 123
    displaying selected styles for, 72
    ThemeRoller settings, 171
configuration
    framework overview, 143–144
    global, 144–148
    page, 149–150
    widgets, 150–152
confirmation.html sample, 56
content
    adding to footers, 69
    adding to headers, 66–69
    aside, 109
    collapsible, 35, 77–78
    dynamic, 157–161
    formatting, 75–80
    shown in columns, 81–82
Content Delivery Networks (CDNs)
    about, 27–29

latest builds, 29
content role, 35, 39
contentTheme property, 149
controlgroup role
    about, 35
    checkboxes and, 138
    grouping, 126–128
    grouping buttons, 84
    radio buttons and, 136
controlgroup widget, 143
CORS (Cross Origin Resource Sharing), 146
count bubbles, 111
create event, 160, 162
creation events, 163
Crockford, Douglas, 202
Cross Origin Resource Sharing (CORS), 146
CSS
    Fireworks support, 179
    jQuery Mobile support, 14
    overflow: property, 147
    position: property, 147
    pseudoclasses, 122
CSS classes, defining in theme files, 180
CSS: position: property, 66
custom data attributes feature (HTML5), 34

D

data-* attributes, 152
data-* namespacing attribute, 145
data-add-back-btn attribute, 41, 52, 66
data-ajax attribute, 49, 116
data-back-btn-text attribute, 41
data-back-btn-theme attribute, 41
data-close-btn-text attribute, 56
data-collapsed attribute, 77, 80
data-content-theme attribute, 78, 79
data-corners attribute, 85
data-count-theme attribute, 112
data-direction attribute, 52, 116
data-dom-cache attribute, 49
data-filter attribute, 113
data-filter-placeholder attribute, 113
data-filter-theme attribute, 113
data-icon attribute
    about, 71, 86
    applying icons to toolbar buttons, 67
    creating custom icons, 87
    interactive rows and, 101
data-iconpos attribute, 88, 89

overflow: property (CSS), 66, 147

P

package definition (offline access)
    about, 183
    accessing online resources, 186
    applicationCache object, 188
    download process, 185
    HTML manifest, 184
    updating resources, 187
packaging for stores
    about, 239
    custom distribution, 241
    packaging with PhoneGap, 242
    preparing packages, 241
    store distribution, 240
page events
    about, 162
    creation events and, 163
    loading events, 163
    showing events, 164
page links
    absolute external, 49
    external, 42, 44–50
    internal, 42–43
    mobile special, 50
page role, 35, 36–39
page utilities, 152–154
page widget, 143
pagebeforechange event, 165
pagebeforecreate event, 163
pagebeforehide event, 165
pagebeforeload event, 163
pagebeforeshow event, 165
pagechange event, 165
pagechangefailed event, 165
pageContainer attribute, 152, 154
pagecreate event, 163
pagehide event, 165
pageinit event, 163
pageload event, 163
pageloadfailed event, 163
pageremove event, 163
pages
    about, 36–39
    caching, 48
    configuration considerations, 149–150
    creating, 157–159
    dialogs and, 52–56

integrating with mobile devices, 57–61
    loading, 149
    navigation between, 40–52
    opening from dialogs, 56
    prefetching, 48
    webapp example, 207–213
pageshow event, 165
pagination plug-in, 228
password text input, 121
path management utilities, 155
pattern attribute, 121
persistent footers, 73
phone calls, 58
PhoneGap Build service, 243
PhoneGap framework
    about, 13
    CDNs and, 27
    packaging with, 242
    webapp preparation and, 26
placeholder attribute, 121
platform utilities, 155
plug-ins
    about, 221
    compatible, 237
    creating, 221–227
    notable, 228–234
    for tablets, 235–237
PNG files, 25, 179
pop transition, 51
position: property (CSS), 66, 147
positioning
    icons, 88
    toolbars, 64–65
prefetching pages, 48
progress event, 189
progressive enhancement technique, 17, 45
pseudo-browsers, 11
pseudoclasses, 122

R

radio buttons, 135
ready event, 141
refresh function, 224
reloadPage property, 154
remote labs, testing webapps, 23
required attribute, 121
Resig, John, 5
resources
    offline, 202

About the Author

Maximiliano Firtman, @firt, is a developer focused on mobile and HTML5 development. He is a trainer in mobile technologies and founder of ITMaster Professional Training. He is the author of many books, including *Programming the Mobile Web* (O'Reilly). He has spoken at international conferences such as OSCON, Velocity, Breaking Development, GOTO Europe, Campus Party, QCon, and Adobe en Vivo.

He has been an Adobe Community Professional since 2011 and a Nokia Developer Champion since 2006, and he has developed many mobile-related projects, such as MobileHTML5.org, MobileTinyURL.com, and iWebInspector.com. He maintains a mobile web development blog at *http://www.mobilexweb.com/*.

He is an expert in native and HTML5 web development, including iOS, Android, PhoneGap, and jQuery technologies.

Colophon

The animal on the cover of *jQuery Mobile: Up and Running* is a Japanese sable (*Martes zibellina brachyurus*). Found on Hokkaido, the northernmost island of Japan, it is one of the many subspecies of the sable, an inhabitant of coniferous forests across Russia and in Mongolia and northern China.

Sables are prized for their soft, silky brown fur. Their pelts have been a staple of the fur trade since the Middle Ages and were a favorite among early modern European royalty. The Russian subspecies are the most highly prized, and the animals are both commercially farmed and hunted wild today.

Sables are 12–18 inches long, not including a 5- to 7-inch tail, and weigh 2–5 pounds. Their fur ranges from light to dark brown and shows a lighter patch on the throat. The Japanese subspecies is distinguished by black markings on its legs and feet.

These omnivorous mammals are crepuscular (active at twilight) and have a varied diet including mammals, birds, fish, eggs, insects, and plants. They may hunt animals larger than themselves—even small deer—and also scavenge other animals' kills. A litter of three pups is born after an eight-month period of delayed implantation (during which the embryos are dormant) and one month of gestation. Sables sometimes interbreed with pine martens, producing a hybrid known as a kidus.

The cover image is from *Wood's Animate Creation*. The cover font is Adobe ITC Garamond. The text font is Linotype Birka; the heading font is Adobe Myriad Condensed; and the code font is LucasFont's TheSansMonoCondensed.

Get even more for your money.

Join the O'Reilly Community, and register the O'Reilly books you own. It's free, and you'll get:

- $4.99 ebook upgrade offer
- 40% upgrade offer on O'Reilly print books
- Membership discounts on books and events
- Free lifetime updates to ebooks and videos
- Multiple ebook formats, DRM FREE
- Participation in the O'Reilly community
- Newsletters
- Account management
- 100% Satisfaction Guarantee

Signing up is easy:

1. **Go to: oreilly.com/go/register**
2. **Create an O'Reilly login.**
3. **Provide your address.**
4. **Register your books.**

Note: English-language books only

To order books online:
oreilly.com/store

For questions about products or an order:
orders@oreilly.com

To sign up to get topic-specific email announcements and/or news about upcoming books, conferences, special offers, and new technologies:
elists@oreilly.com

For technical questions about book content:
booktech@oreilly.com

To submit new book proposals to our editors:
proposals@oreilly.com

O'Reilly books are available in multiple DRM-free ebook formats. For more information:
oreilly.com/ebooks

Spreading the knowledge of innovators	oreilly.com

Have it your way.

O'Reilly eBooks

- Lifetime access to the book when you buy through oreilly.com
- Provided in up to four DRM-free file formats, for use on the devices of your choice: PDF, .epub, Kindle-compatible .mobi, and Android .apk
- Fully searchable, with copy-and-paste and print functionality
- Alerts when files are updated with corrections and additions

oreilly.com/ebooks/

Safari Books Online

- Access the contents and quickly search over 7000 books on technology, business, and certification guides
- Learn from expert video tutorials, and explore thousands of hours of video on technology and design topics
- Download whole books or chapters in PDF format, at no extra cost, to print or read on the go
- Get early access to books as they're being written
- Interact directly with authors of upcoming books
- Save up to 35% on O'Reilly print books

See the complete Safari Library at safari.oreilly.com

O'REILLY®

Lightning Source UK Ltd.
Milton Keynes UK
UKOW020307070612

193947UK00004B/11/P